FIELD OF HONOR
How Flight 93 Inspired a Nation

Richard Snodgrass of Pittsburgh looks to the United Flight 93 crash site just after dawn on August 18, 2006, during one of several visits he made to the temporary memorial. "There is a real power to this place," he said.
GUY WATHEN

EDITOR
FRANK L. CRAIG

CONTRIBUTING EDITORS
JAMES CUDDY, JR.
RICHARD A. MONTI
SANDRA TOLLIVER

SUPERVISING EDITOR
SANDRA SKOWRON

CREATIVE DIRECTOR
JAMES M. KUBUS

DESIGNER
ELIZABETH KANE JACKSON

PROJECT MANAGER
CAROL SHREFLER

WRITERS
MARY PICKELS
JENNIFER REEGER
CRAIG SMITH
MIKE WERESCHAGIN

PHOTO EDITORS
JUSTIN MERRIMAN
GUY WATHEN

PHOTOGRAPHERS
BRIAN F. HENRY
KEITH HODAN
CHRISTOPHER HORNER
BARRY REEGER
JOHN C. SCHISLER
ERIC SCHMADEL
SCOTT SPANGLER
SEAN STIPP
JARED WICKERHAM

COPY EDITOR
CHARLES RONDINELLI

GRAPHIC ARTIST
JASON LANZA

PHOTO TECHNICIAN
JACK FORDYCE

*Copyright © 2011
by Trib Total Media, Inc.*

TRIB | TOTAL MEDIA

*Pittsburgh Tribune-Review
503 Martindale Street
Pittsburgh, Pennsylvania 15212*

Richard M. Scaife Publisher, Inc.

All rights reserved. No part of this book may be reproduced in any form or by any electronic, mechanical or other means, now known or hereafter invented, including xerography, photocopying, recording, or information storage and retrieval systems without permission in writing by the publisher, except by a reviewer who may quote brief passages in a review.

ISBN 978-0-9819589-5-8

*'Field of Honor: How Flight 93 Inspired a Nation'
was printed in Pittsburgh, Pennsylvania by Knepper Press*

CONTENTS

III FOREWORD V

CHAPTER ONE **III** THE DEFINING TRUTH 1

CHAPTER TWO **III** THE FIRST BATTLEFIELD 15

CHAPTER THREE **III** HEROES ALL 26

CHAPTER FOUR **III** INSPIRATION & MEMORY 69

CHAPTER FIVE **III** 'WE WILL FIND YOU' 87

CHAPTER SIX **III** JUSTICE IS DONE 95

EPILOGUE **III** FIELD OF HONOR 97

III ACKNOWLEDGEMENTS 105

III REFERENCES & SOURCES 106

FOREWORD
BY GORDON W. FELT
YOUNGEST BROTHER OF FLIGHT 93 PASSENGER EDWARD P. FELT

THE EVENTS THAT UNFOLDED ON SEPTEMBER 11, 2001, FOREVER WILL HAUNT OUR NATION. THE VIOLENCE OF GLOBAL TERRORISM CAUGHT US OFF GUARD AND UNPREPARED TO PROCESS EVENTS THAT, UNTIL THAT DAY, WE SAW AS IMAGES ON TV, ONLINE OR IN THE MOVIES, BUT NOT ON OUR SHORES.

The terrorists viciously attacked our country's greatest financial and military symbols and killed thousands of innocent people. As this was happening, 40 passengers and crew members aboard United Flight 93 — aware of the events taking place in New York and Washington — refused to be overwhelmed by the horror they faced, and consciously spent their final 35 minutes altering the course of history.

We know that these men and women prayed together. We know that they discussed a plan to retake the plane and then voted to take action. We know that they stormed the cockpit. In standing up to those who brought evil to our shores, the 40 brave men and women of Flight 93 lost their lives fighting. In doing so, the 9/11 Commission determined that they saved the United States Capitol, one of our nation's greatest symbols of democracy. Their story will stand the test of time and inspire generations to come.

The Flight 93 National Memorial will stand as a beacon, inspiring those who visit. It will honor the passengers and crew of Flight 93 as individuals, as well as their collective actions heroically played out in the sky over southwestern Pennsylvania on one of our nation's darkest days. It will tell the story of a community deeply affected by the events of September 11th and how its residents came together as first responders and then ambassadors, preserving the dignity of those who were lost and the sanctity of their story.

Gordon W. Felt is president of Families of Flight 93 and a commissioner on the Flight 93 Federal Advisory Commission.

Hailing from central New York, Gordon and his wife Donna own and operate Camp Northwood, a residential summer camp for high-functioning autistic and learning-challenged children.

Gordon's involvement in the Flight 93 National Memorial project began in December 2002 as an original board member of Families of Flight 93.

CHAPTER ONE
THE DEFINING TRUTH

MUCH OF WHO WE WERE ON SEPTEMBER 10, 2001, PROVED TO BE EITHER TOO RESILIENT OR TOO STUBBORN TO DISAPPEAR WITH THE SMOKE THAT ROSE OVER LOWER MANHATTAN, THE PENTAGON AND SOMERSET COUNTY ON SEPTEMBER 11.

Changes that came to the homeland have been relatively small — metal detectors in public buildings that didn't have them before, more frequent requirements to show our photo IDs, and more thorough checks of our bodies and luggage in airports. We pushed against the legal definitions of torture, detention and assassination, but abandoned neither our Constitution nor our courts when they pushed back. We plunged into recession and deficit spending, but did not abandon our economic system. We broadened the power of intelligence gatherers, but continue to seek protections for our privacy.

We have not rationed gasoline or nylon, nor swept aside gender barriers to ensure our factories continue to produce, as we did after Pearl Harbor. Tens of millions have not joined our military, though more than 3 million did. Our concerns in the still-untouched early hours of September 11, 2001, align with those of today: We wondered whether unemployment would go down and whether budget deficits would go up.

But we weren't looking where we should have been. Two days before 9/11, Ahmad Shah Massoud, the Afghan warlord who united the Northern Alliance against the Taliban, was assassinated; his death didn't make newspaper front pages. Defense Secretary Donald Rumsfeld, vowing to cut his department's budget, said on September 10: "Today, we declare war on bureaucracy."

> "Today, we've had a national tragedy. Two airplanes have crashed into the World Trade Center in an apparent terrorist attack on our country. I ... have ordered that the full resources of the federal government go to help the victims and their families and to conduct a full-scale investigation to hunt down and to find those folks who committed this act."
>
> **PRESIDENT GEORGE W. BUSH**
> IN REMARKS TO THE NATION AT 9:30 A.M., SEPTEMBER 11, 2001. SEVEN MINUTES LATER, AMERICAN AIRLINES FLIGHT 77 CRASHED INTO THE PENTAGON AND 33 MINUTES LATER, UNITED AIRLINES FLIGHT 93 CRASHED.

Headlines from the Tribune-Review's September 12, 2001, edition tell the story of the 9/11 terror attacks. The newspaper produces a 16-page extra edition (bottom right) within hours after the first plane struck the North Tower of the World Trade Center at 8:46:40 a.m.

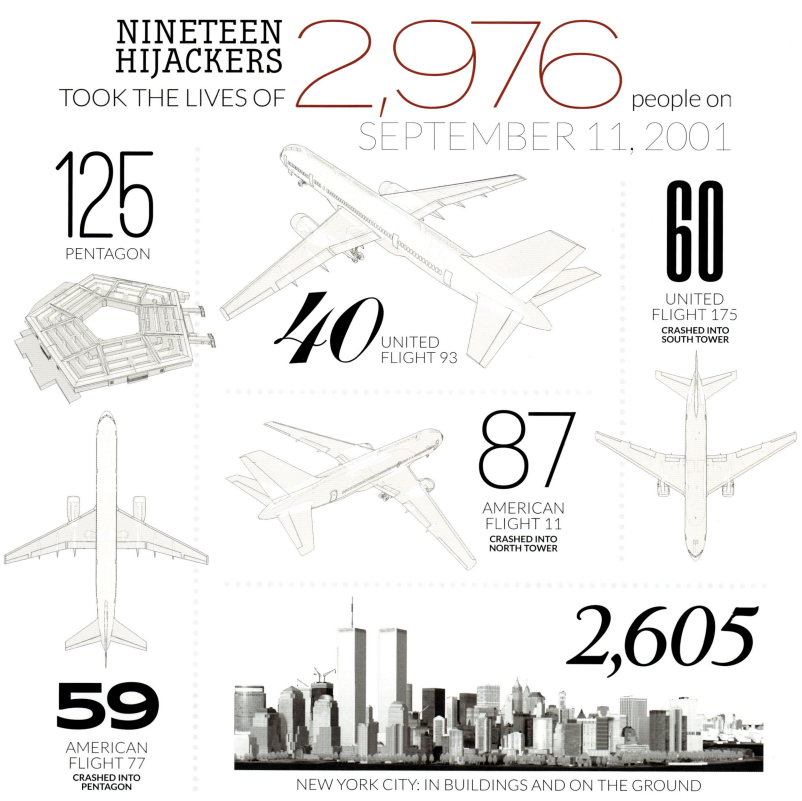

GUY WATHEN

The tolling of a bell — once for each of the 40 Flight 93 passengers and crew members — becomes a traditional part of annual memorial services held near the crash site. This bell-ringing is part of the service on September 11, 2005.

The following morning, Hurricane Erin moved toward the East Coast as 19 Middle Eastern terrorists slipped through the last layers of security between us and their consuming hatred.

They hijacked American Airlines Flight 11 first, then United Airlines 175 and then American Airlines 77. Hijackers working in teams of five slashed at their victims with box cutters and wrapped their hands around the controls in the cockpits. Flight 11 flew southward, through an unblemished, azure sky, into the North Tower of the World Trade Center. Sixteen minutes and 31 seconds later, with the world watching, Flight 175 passed over the Statue of Liberty and slammed into the South Tower, and we knew this was an attack. Half an hour later, Flight 77 rammed into the hard stone of the Pentagon.

United Airlines Flight 93 was the last plane, and its final moments did not belong to the enemy. The four hijackers knew they were losing control, and took the plane down into a field near Shanksville, Pennsylvania — a field that became one of sorrow and loss and defiance and rebellion and sacrifice.

The attacks of September 11 claimed nearly 3,000 lives in America, but the most dramatic transformations occurred overseas. Wars reached into Afghanistan's valleys, Iraq's streets, Yemen's deserts and the cities of Pakistan, where more than nine years of hunting by two administrations culminated in a daring raid and the death of Osama bin Laden on May 1, 2011. Popular uprisings across the Middle East and North Africa deposed dictators and unsettled long-standing power structures.

Our role in those transformations divided us. We require of our children no military service, and so only a few have borne the sacrifice. But our divisions aren't new. America demands no common prayers. Our unity remains rooted in our principles and in the truths we hold to be self-evident.

Perhaps the defining truth of the final act of the 40 men and women who fought to retake Flight 93 is this: They died trying to preserve life, not take it. And so we toll bells for the lost, and mark the anniversaries of their deaths to bridge the time that has passed. We dedicate fields to their memory, and in our finest moments, we rededicate ourselves to that which gave their lives enduring meaning.

OUT OF THE CLEAR SKY TRAGEDY ARRIVES

The terrorist attacks of September 11, 2001, claimed nearly 3,000 lives. Key events as the day unfolded:

7:59 a.m.
American Airlines Flight 11 leaves Boston's Logan International Airport for California carrying 92 people.

8:14
United Airlines Flight 175 leaves Boston with 65 people.

Flight 11 is hijacked about now.

8:20
American Airlines Flight 77 leaves Washington Dulles International Airport in Chantilly, Virginia, with 64 people aboard.

8:42
United Airlines Flight 93 leaves Newark International Airport in New Jersey with 44 people.

8:42-8:46
The hijacking of Flight 175 occurs.

8:46
The North American Aerospace Defense Command's Northeast Air Defense Sector scrambles fighter jets to find Flight 11.

8:46:40
Flight 11 crashes into the North Tower of the World Trade Center, killing all aboard and cutting through floors 93 to 99. The crash kills hundreds of people in the building and traps hundreds more. New York City police and firefighters and police from The Port Authority of New York & New Jersey race to the burning tower. **1**

8:50
President George W. Bush, during a scheduled visit of the Emma E. Booker Elementary School in Sarasota, Florida, is told by White House Chief of Staff Andrew Card that a plane crashed into the World Trade Center. **1**

8:51-8:54
The hijacking of Flight 77 occurs.

9:00
The Fire Department of New York, the New York Police Department and the Port Authority Police Department are at their highest mobilization levels. All on-duty World Trade Center response staff are mobilized.

9:03:11
Flight 175 crashes into the South Tower of the World Trade Center, slicing through floors 77 to 85. **2**

9:05
Bush is told a second plane crashed into the World Trade Center.

9:15
Officials begin closing New York City bridges and tunnels to all but emergency vehicles.

9:17
The Federal Aviation Administration orders New York airports to close.

9:24
Fighter jets from Langley Air Force base in Virginia are scrambled to find Flight 11 in the belief it is heading to Washington.

9:25
The FAA's Herndon Command Center orders the first-ever nationwide groundstop, prohibiting flight take-offs. Incoming transatlantic flights are diverted to Canada.

9:28
The hijackers attack Flight 93, which is flying at 35,000 feet over eastern Ohio.

PHOTOS BY AP IMAGES

9:30
The New York Stock Exchange does not open; its employees evacuate.

9:30
Bush makes his first public comments: "Today, we've had a national tragedy."

9:37:46
Flight 77 crashes into the Pentagon. **3**

9:40
The FAA orders 4,565 planes in North American airspace to land at the nearest airports. For the first time in the nation's history, the agency halts all flight operations.

9:45
Evacuations are under way at the White House, the United States Capitol, the Empire State Building, the United Nations, the Kennedy Space Center and other sites in the United States. Bush heads to an Air Force base in Louisiana.

9:52
Flight 93 passes a few miles south of Pittsburgh.

9:57
A warning of imminent collapse is issued for the damaged portion of the Pentagon.

9:58
A 911 operator in Westmoreland County receives a cell phone call from Flight 93 passenger Edward Felt, saying the plane is being hijacked.

9:58-10:00
Vice President Dick Cheney is told the Air Force is trying to establish a combat air patrol over Washington.

9:59
South Tower collapses after burning for 56 minutes. The collapse takes 10 seconds and kills approximately 600 workers and first responders in the building and area. **4**

10:03:11
Flight 93 crashes near Shanksville as passengers and crew fight for control of the plane.

10:10-10:15
Cheney gives authorization during this time to shoot down Flight 93, believed to be 80 miles from Washington, saying he spoke with the president.

10:13
Evacuation of the United Nations is under way.

10:15
The damaged section of the Pentagon's E Ring, the outermost ring of the office complex, collapses.

10:12-10:18
Cheney for the second time gives authorization to shoot down Flight 93, believed to be 60 miles from Washington.

10:20
Bush's press secretary Ari Fleischer records that the president tells him that he authorized shooting down Flight 93, if necessary.

10:28
World Trade Center's North Tower collapses, after burning 102 minutes. The collapse takes 11 seconds and kills approximately 1,400 people, including firefighters, workers and tourists. **1**

JUSTIN LANE PHOTOGRAPHY

Walkiria Monteiro of Brazil reacts to a news report just after the North Tower collapse. She and others watched television from inside Carnegie Mellon University's Graduate School of Industrial Administration.

JOHN C. SCHISLER

THE WHITE HOUSE

People coated with dust from the collapse of the World Trade Center flee lower Manhattan. Jonathan Markowitz, second from the left, a Chicago commodities broker, was on the 85th floor of the North Tower when American Airlines Flight 11 slammed into the building.
AP IMAGES

10:30
Hundreds of thousands of people covered in white dust and soot flee lower Manhattan. New York Governor George E. Pataki declares a state of emergency. **1**

1:04 p.m.
Bush addresses the nation from Barksdale Air Force Base in Louisiana. The military is on "high alert." Once the president leaves Louisiana, he will fly to an Air Force base in Nebraska. Officials are not sure he would be safe returning to Washington.

1:27
A state of emergency is declared in Washington.

1:44
Ships leave Norfolk, Virginia, to protect the East Coast from attack.

3:55
Bush conducts a national security meeting by phone from Offutt Air Force Base in Nebraska.

4:01
News reports cite federal officials saying there are "good indications" that Osama bin Laden, suspected in bombing of USS Cole, is involved in these attacks.

4:36
Bush departs Offutt Air Force Base for Washington. Aboard Air Force One, he prepares a speech to the nation for the evening. **2**

5:20
The 47-story 7 World Trade Center collapses. Later, the North Bridge and St. Nicholas Church collapse. The Marriott Hotel has collapsed; 4, 5 and 6 World Trade Center are partially collapsed.

5:30
U.S. officials confirm Flight 93 could have been headed for Camp David in Maryland, the White House or U.S. Capitol.

6:40
Secretary of Defense Donald Rumsfeld, who was in the Pentagon when the plane hit, says the building will be open the following morning.

6:55
Bush arrives at the White House on Marine One after landing at Andrews Air Force Base in Maryland, escorted by fighter jets.

8:30
Bush speaks to the nation, stating "thousands of lives were suddenly ended by evil." He says the United States will make no distinction between the terrorists who committed these acts and those who harbor them.

9:55
New York Mayor Rudy Giuliani closes New York City schools for the following day and declares the city has all the volunteers it can handle for rescue efforts. There is no evidence of airborne chemical agents, officials say.

11:29
Pataki inspects Ground Zero.

Sources: The 9/11 Report; The National September 11 Memorial and Museum; The Port Authority of New York & New Jersey; New York State Museum; Department of Defense; Tribune-Review.

Lower Manhattan smolders early in the morning of September 12. By then, New York City had all the volunteers it could handle for rescue efforts.
GUY WATHEN

"These acts shatter steel, but they cannot dent the steel of American resolve."

PRESIDENT GEORGE W. BUSH
September 11, 2001

CHAPTER TWO
THE FIRST BATTLEFIELD

FOR MOST OF ITS EXISTENCE, THE SOMERSET COUNTY TOWN OF SHANKSVILLE, SAID THE LATE MAYOR ERNEST STULL, WAS A PLACE BETWEEN HERE AND NOWHERE.

That changed when United Airlines Flight 93 plowed into a field less than two miles away. The Shanksville Volunteer Fire Department sent the first rescuers, who found only a crater in a windswept, Stonycreek Township field that was once a strip mine.

Residents realize how close they came to an even bigger disaster. The plane crashed only seven seconds away from town by air.

Before 9/11, people in Shanksville knew their neighbors. The murder of 40 people aboard Flight 93 brought strangers to town: investigators and members of media; dignitaries and family of passengers and crew; and then people from across the country and around the world who wanted to see the place where Americans fought the first battle in the war against terror.

Shanksville residents put out welcome mats for everyone. They opened their homes to family members of Flight 93 passengers and crew. When the town's roads became clogged with cars, motorcycles and buses carrying outsiders, they did not complain and instead offered directions.

They serve as ambassadors at the memorial. They will not let anyone forget.

> "You just don't expect something like this to happen in a town the size of Shanksville."
>
> **BOB PAGE**
> EYEWITNESS
> *September 11, 2001*

Troopers with the Pennsylvania State Police Tactical Mounted Unit await the arrival of United States Attorney General John Ashcroft on September 20, 2001. Ashcroft toured the Flight 93 crash site with FBI Director Robert Mueller. Shortly after they left, families of the passengers and crew visited the place where their loved ones died.
SEAN STIPP

UNITED AIRLINES FLIGHT 93'S FINAL FLIGHT

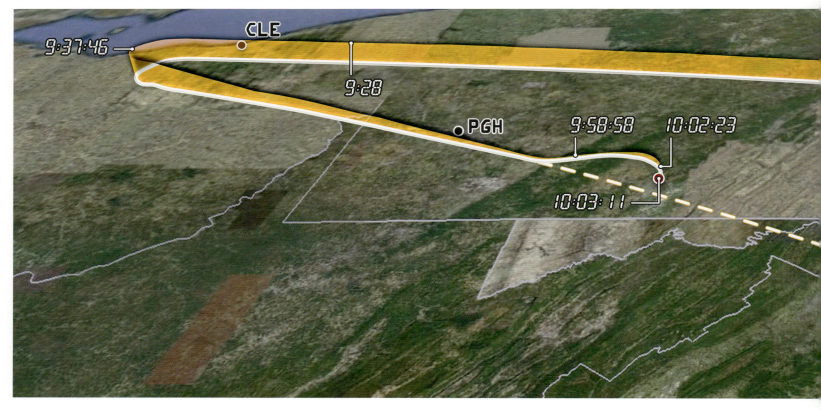

7:03-7:39 a.m.
Saeed al Ghamdi, Ahmed al Nami, Ahmad al Haznawi and Ziad Jarrah check in at United Airlines ticket counter at Newark International Airport.

7:39-7:48
Hijackers board United Airlines Flight 93, seated in first class.

8:14
American Airlines Flight 11, en route from Boston to Los Angeles, is hijacked about now.

8:42
Flight 93 takes off, bound for San Francisco, carrying 44 people. Its scheduled 8 a.m. departure was delayed because of the airport's heavy morning traffic.

8:42-8:46
United Airlines Flight 175, en route from Boston to Los Angeles, is hijacked.

8:46:40
Flight 11 crashes into the North Tower of the World Trade Center, cutting through floors 93 to 99.

8:51-8:54
American Airlines Flight 77, en route from Washington to Los Angeles, is hijacked.

9:03:11
Flight 175 crashes into the South Tower of the World Trade Center, slicing through floors 77 to 85.

9:23
United Airlines flight dispatcher Ed Ballinger tells Flight 93 to beware of cockpit intrusions and that two aircraft hit the World Trade Center.

9:26
Flight 93 Pilot Jason Dahl asks Ballinger to confirm the message.

9:28
The hijackers attack Flight 93, traveling at 35,000 feet over eastern Ohio. The plane suddenly drops 700 feet. The Federal Aviation Administration's air traffic control center in Cleveland receives radio transmissions from either the captain or first officer: "Mayday," amid sounds of a struggle; then, "Hey, get out of here — get out of here — get out of here." Passengers and crew begin making calls on air phones and cell phones, providing vital information to people on the ground and to passengers.

9:31:58
A hijacker, believed to be Jarrah, announces: "Ladies and gentlemen: Here the captain, please sit down keep remaining seating. We have a bomb on board. So sit."

9:35:25-9:36
A woman, likely a flight attendant, struggles and pleads for her life. She is killed or silenced.

9:37:46
Flight 77 crashes into the Pentagon.

9:39
The FAA's Cleveland Air Route Traffic Control Center overhears this announcement from Flight 93: "Ah! Here's the captain; I would like you all to remain seated. We have a bomb aboard, and we are going back to the airport, and we have our demands. So, please remain quiet." Jarrah apparently didn't know how to operate the communication radios, so this message went out on the air traffic control channel. The passengers apparently did not hear it.

Sources: The 9/11 Report; The National Transportation Safety Board; National Park Service; Tribune-Review; FBI transcript of the cockpit voice recorder from Flight 93; Google Earth.

9:41
The Flight 93 transponder is turned off.

9:57
Passengers and crew begin their assault on hijackers. Flight Attendant Sandy Waugh Bradshaw ends a telephone call to her husband, Philip, saying everyone was running up to first class and she had to go.

9:58
A 911 operator in Westmoreland County receives a cell phone call from Flight 93 passenger Edward Felt saying the plane is being hijacked.

9:58:58
Jarrah tells another hijacker in the cockpit to block the door. He rolls the plane sharply to the left and right. Passengers keep fighting. The cockpit voice recorder captures sounds of loud thumps, crashes, shouts and breaking glasses and plates.

10:00:03
Jarrah stabilizes the plane.

10:00:08
Jarrah asks, "Is that it? Shall we finish it off?" A hijacker responds, "No. Not yet." A hijacker says: "When they all come, we finish it off." Sounds of fighting continue outside the cockpit. Jarrah pitches the nose of the aircraft up and down.

10:00:26
A male passenger says, "In the cockpit. If we don't, we'll die."

10:00:42
An unidentified passenger yells, "Roll it."

10:01
About now Jarrah stops violent maneuvers. "Allah is the greatest! Allah is the greatest!" he says, and then asks, "Is that it? I mean, shall we pull it down?" Another hijacker replies, "Yes, put it in it, and pull it down."

10:02:23
Passengers and crew keep up their assault. A hijacker says: "Pull it down! Pull it down! *Down!*" The plane begins a rapid descent, then rolls onto its back.

10:03:03
A hijacker shouts: "Allah is the greatest! Allah is the greatest!"

10:03:11
With sounds of passengers and crew fighting, Flight 93 crashes into a field near Shanksville at 580 miles per hour, about 20 minutes flying time from Washington.

10:10-10:15
During this time, Vice President Dick Cheney gives authorization to shoot down Flight 93, believed to be 80 miles from Washington, saying he spoke with President George W. Bush.

10:12-10:18
Cheney gives second authorization to shoot down Flight 93, believed to be 60 miles from Washington. In the next minutes, word arrives that Flight 93 crashed in Pennsylvania.

10:20
Bush's press secretary Ari Fleischer records the president tells him that he authorized shooting down Flight 93 if necessary.

10:30
About now the White House gets word of an aircraft five to 10 miles from Washington. Cheney authorizes shooting it down, but officials learn it is a medical helicopter.

"We couldn't tell what we were looking at. There's just a huge crater in the woods."

NICK TWEARDY
OF STONYCREEK, WHO
RUSHED TO THE CRASH
SITE HOPING TO HELP.

September 11, 2001

Mark Stahl of Somerset, Pennsylvania, holds his photograph of a smoldering field near Shanksville taken minutes after United Airlines Flight 93 crashed there.
JUSTIN MERRIMAN

After a boom nearly knocked her off her couch the morning of September 11, 2001, Val McClatchey grabbed her camera, stepped onto the front porch of her Somerset County home and shot one frame of a cloud of smoke rising from the wreckage of Flight 93. Her photograph is thought to be the earliest one of the crash. She originally thought a small plane went down. When she heard the sirens, she knew the accident was far worse.

KEITH HODAN

SEAN STIPP

Federal evidence technicians search the area surrounding the crater. Of the four planes used in the 9/11 attacks, only Flight 93's voice recorder and flight data recorder were recovered, and both yielded information.

A charred stock report that apparently was aboard the plane was found in New Baltimore, Pennsylvania, six miles from site. Hunter Stoe, then 3, found it and a signed check as he helped his father, Andy, with trash.

SCOTT SPANGLER

FBI aerial photo taken September 19, 2001.
FBI | AP IMAGES

SCOTT SPANGLER

Stonycreek farmers watch a Pennsylvania State Police helicopter circle a Somerset County field on September 14, 2001, during a search for evidence from the crash of Flight 93. David Scott, in the plaid shirt, said FBI agents tagged cornstalks where they found evidence.

United States Representative John Murtha toured the site on the day after the crash. "When you have fanatics willing to commit suicide, it's impossible to predict where they're going to hit," he said. Murtha represented a portion of Somerset County in Congress. He died in 2010.

SCOTT SPANGLER

The Reverend James Simons, rector of St. Michael's of the Valley Episcopal Church in Ligonier, prays near the Flight 93 crash site on September 11, 2001. The plane flew low and over his church before crashing minutes later. Simons managed to get to the impact area and said he was astonished by how small the crater was.

Members of the Pennsylvania Army National Guard make their way to the site.

Lee Purbaugh, sitting, and his mother, Lucy Menear recount the crash of Flight 93 to reporters on September 11, 2001, from their home, about 1,500 yards from the crash site. Menear said she was in her living room watching TV when she heard what sounded like thunder. When she saw "18 or 20" fire trucks heading down the road, "I knew there was something wrong."

Pennsylvania State Police protect the Somerset County field where United Flight 93 went down.
JUSTIN MERRIMAN

"The entire community of Shanksville and the coroner and all the volunteers at the flight 93 center are some of my biggest heroes, because I think the way they handled such sensitive subject matter is really to be commended."

LYZ GLICK BEST
WIFE OF FLIGHT 93 PASSENGER JEREMY GLICK

April 12, 2011

CHAPTER THREE
HEROES ALL

UNITED FLIGHT 93 CARRIED 40 PASSENGERS AND CREW MEMBERS, ABOARD A PLANE WITH A SEATING CAPACITY FOR 182, WHEN IT TOOK OFF FROM NEWARK INTERNATIONAL AIRPORT ON SEPTEMBER 11, 2001, BUT TOGETHER, THEY POSSESSED AN INCREDIBLE ASSORTMENT OF TALENT.

Among the passengers was a businessman who was a pilot; a man who was a judo champion in college; a former United States Army paratrooper; a 6-foot-5-inch rugby player; a law enforcement officer with the United States Fish and Wildlife Service; and a former police officer-turned-flight attendant, whom one colleague described as one tough cookie.

There were college students and retirees, people traveling for business or vacations, and people heading home.

Many of them weren't supposed to be on United Flight 93. They were booked on other flights, but switched travel plans.

A cockpit voice recorder shows that 46 minutes after the Boeing 575 took off, four terrorists took over the plane. Some passengers and crew members used cell phones or air phones to contact family members. They learned about the other horrors of 9/11, said their good-byes and set out to take back Flight 93.

They fought to the end — heroes all.

A bronze plaque in their honor hangs at the United States Capitol, believed to have been the terrorists' target.

> "The men and women of Flight 93 were brave in a way few of us will ever be called upon to be."
>
> **LYNNE CHENEY**
> WIFE OF VICE PRESIDENT DICK CHENEY
> *September 20, 2001*

Christian Adams

HOMETOWN: Biebelsheim, Rheinland-Pfalz, Germany /// AGE: 37 /// OCCUPATION: Deputy director, German Wine Institute
FAMILY: Wife, Silke; children, Lukas and Theresa

Christian Adams never took a backseat when it came to work.

As deputy director of the German Wine Institute, a quasi-government body that promotes German wines, Adams could have let others do the heavy lifting at wine tastings and other events. But he always needed to be doing something.

"He would just come to me and say, 'What do you need? What do you want me to do now?'" said Carol Sullivan, who helped promote German wines in the United States through the German Wine Information Bureau. "There was no ego. There was no sense of 'This is who I am and this is who you are.'"

After he earned a degree in the study of wines and wine making from Geisenheim Grape Breeding Institute, the leading wine making school in Germany, he came to America to pursue a marketing degree from the University of California at Davis. He finished his studies in 1989 and got a job in the export department of the German Wine Institute.

Christian was diplomatic and quick to laugh. He helped his wife Silke run her family's winery. Usually, he would be working there in late September when vintage tastings typically were held in the United States. But in 2001, the tastings were held earlier in the month, enabling Christian to attend.

Christian was in the United States for two wine-tasting events. He was traveling from New York, where the first event was held, to help set up the second event in San Francisco.

Lorraine Bay

HOMETOWN: East Windsor, New Jersey /// AGE: 58 /// OCCUPATION: Flight attendant, United Airlines
FAMILY: Husband, Erich; cousin, Ed Root

Lorraine Bay never let a special occasion pass without sending a card. So it wasn't a surprise that, a few days after 9/11, some of her fellow flight attendants received cards she mailed just before her death.

Lorraine, who had no children, enjoyed mentoring young flight attendants. After 37 years working for United Airlines, she was one of the airline's most senior flight attendants based at Newark International Airport.

Her smile and the ease with which she talked to people made her good at her job. She loved meeting people — both regular Joes and famous folks, such as President Ronald Reagan. Her husband, Erich, said she was never late for the job she loved.

Despite busy work schedules, they made sure Fridays were date nights. Lorraine didn't like it when he bought a motorcycle, but rode on it with him anyway.

"She tolerated my nonsense," he said.

When she left for work on September 11, Lorraine promised her husband they would celebrate his upcoming birthday the next day, before he was to leave on a business trip.

Months later, hidden in her closet and drawers, Erich Bay found presents his wife wanted to give him — belts, ties and shirts.

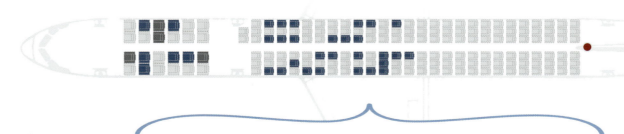

Lorraine chose Flight 93 because of her preference for nonstop, coast-to-coast flights so she would get a lot of flying hours in a short period of time.

Todd M. Beamer

HOMETOWN: Cranbury, New Jersey /// AGE: 32 /// OCCUPATION: Account manager, Oracle Corporation
FAMILY: Wife, Lisa; sons, David Paul and Andrew Todd; daughter, Morgan Kay, born after his death; parents, David and Peggy Beamer; sisters, Melissa Wilson and Michele Sorensen

Todd Beamer was just starting to pass along his love for baseball to his older son, David, in the summer of 2001.

Todd played baseball throughout his youth and at California State University at Fresno and Wheaton College in Illinois. That summer he was coaching 3-year-old David.

"Step and throw," he'd tell his son. "Step and throw."

"I really miss the fact that he's not there for them," said Todd's father, David Beamer. "They're good baseball players. They'd be better if their dad was around coaching them."

Todd's family was a priority — to the point that he remained in sales because a promotion to management might have uprooted his family.

Todd really listened to people. One of the last calls he made before boarding United Airlines Flight 93 was to a friend looking for a new job. Todd wanted to check in to see how things were going.

His sales accomplishments earned him a trip to Italy with his wife Lisa. They returned to New Jersey on September 10, and he was flying to California the next morning. He would catch the red-eye back to New Jersey that night and planned to eat breakfast with his wife and kids on September 12.

He is credited with saying, "Let's roll," before the passenger revolt.

Todd was traveling to California for a business meeting and planned to return to New Jersey that night.

Alan Anthony Beaven

HOMETOWN: Oakland, California /// AGE: 48 /// OCCUPATION: Environmental attorney, Berman DeValerio Pease Tabacco Burt & Pucillo
FAMILY: Wife, Kimi; sons, John and Chris; daughter, Sonali

Alan Beaven practiced law in his native New Zealand, in England and in New York, but it wasn't until he arrived in California that he found his passion. He began pursuing environmental cases, particularly those involving the Clean Water Act.

"He really kind of took it to heart," said his son, John Beaven. "He wanted to pursue something he was passionate about and wanted to make a difference."

Alan lived simply. He liked comfortable clothes and being in the outdoors. Family was important to him. When his first marriage broke up and his sons were moving to California with their mom, he moved there, too, so he could stay close to his boys. He loved kids — his own, his friends' children and those in the neighborhood who flocked to his house to play.

"He was just very approachable, and I think a large part of it was because he didn't treat kids like kids. He treated them like an individual," his son said.

Alan lived in the moment. He took vacations on a whim. He disapproved of worrying about tomorrow. In the days after his death, a note was found posted on the wall of his temporary office in upstate New York.

"Fear. Who Cares?" it said.

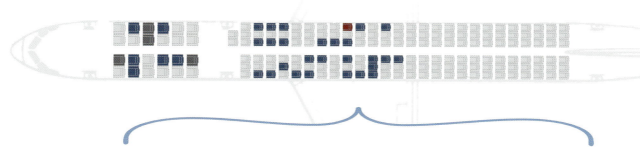

Alan lived with his wife and daughter in upstate New York while they prepared to go to India for a one-year volunteer trip to work on environmental issues. He was returning to California to finish work on a case.

Mark Kendall Bingham

HOMETOWN: San Francisco /// AGE: 31 /// OCCUPATION: Founder and CEO, The Bingham Group
FAMILY: Mother, Alice Hoagland; father, Gerald W. Bingham; grandfather, Herbert Hoglan; uncles, Vaughn and Lee Hoglan; and aunts, Candyce and Cathy Hoglan

Mark Bingham seemed to spend the final months of his life as if he knew they were his last. On a trip to Hawaii with friends, he jumped off cliffs into the ocean. He ran with the bulls in Pamplona, Spain.

"In many ways, Mark taught me how to live my life, and I'm still learning from his example," said his mother, Alice Hoagland.

Mark was a shy, self-conscious boy who grew into a strong, confident young man after he was introduced to rugby in high school. He played the sport at the University of California, Berkeley, where he was a member of two national championship teams.

He made friends easily. His ease in social situations led to work in public relations firms in the San Francisco area until he organized his own public relations company in 1999.

A gay man, Mark helped found two gay rugby teams that welcomed all minorities. After his death, the International Gay Rugby Association and Board's biennial international rugby competition was christened the Bingham Cup in his honor. A daredevil and defender of the underdog, Mark got himself injured quite a few times.

"His last words before he was loaded into an ambulance were always, 'Don't tell my mom,'" Alice Hoagland said.

Mark was commuting between his New York and San Francisco offices and preparing to attend the wedding of a close friend.

Deora Frances Bodley

HOMETOWN: San Diego, California /// AGE: 20 /// OCCUPATION: Student, Santa Clara University
FAMILY: Mother, Deborah Borza; sister, Murial Borza; stepfather, Marc Borza; stepmother, Nancy Bodley; grandfather, Francis Guerra; uncles, Kevin Guerra and Walt Bodley; aunts, Christine Abbott and Dianne Baker. Her father, Derrill Bodley, died in 2005.

From a young age, Deora Frances Bodley could look past people's faults. In her journal, she wrote about her friends and how she loved them, warts and all.

"She loved them for who they were and who they weren't," said her mother, Deborah Borza.

Deora was the youngest person aboard United Flight 93. In high school, she educated other students about AIDS and HIV. She helped care for animals at a shelter in San Diego, California.

As a college student, she mentored children in an after-school reading program. Her parents' divorce influenced her into studying to become a child psychologist.

"She figured, 'What if I provided assistance for other young kids going through the same thing,'" Borza said.

Her sister, Murial, was 10 years younger but they were incredibly close. After Deora's high school basketball games, she scooped up her sister and took her into the locker room with the team.

Her closest friends called her "Buddha," a nickname derived from her last name. To everyone else, she was Deora — a name her parents chose because they liked "Leora" but wanted a name that began with a "D" like theirs.

Only later did they discover Deora is the Gaelic word for tears.

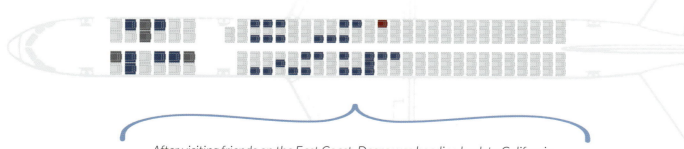

After visiting friends on the East Coast, Deora was heading back to California. Scheduled to take a later flight, she switched to Flight 93 so the friend taking her to the airport would not be late for her college classes.

Sandy Waugh Bradshaw

HOMETOWN: Greensboro, North Carolina /// AGE: 38 /// OCCUPATION: Flight attendant, United Airlines
FAMILY: Husband, Phil; daughter, Alexandria; son, Nathan; stepdaughter, Shenan; mother, Pat Waugh; sisters, Debbie Waugh, Sharon Liles and Tracy Peele; brother, Rod Waugh

Sandy Waugh Bradshaw loved growing up on her parents' North Carolina farm.

She worked in the chicken house, raised a calf and kept her own horse. But, as she grew older, she longed for a career in the sky.

Sandy had not flown much as a girl. After working secretarial jobs to build up her resume, she got her shot with US Airways as a flight attendant in 1990. When the airline laid her off a few months later, she landed a job with United Airlines.

"She liked the traveling around," said her mother, Pat Waugh. "Even after she had children, she didn't want to give up the job. Even though she was a very attentive mother, she still enjoyed flying."

Sandy was a planner, a take-charge person. She was easygoing in many ways, but if pushed, she'd express herself. Strong and feisty, she once caught some guys trying to steal her brother's three-wheeler and drove after them five or six miles to get their license plate number.

She loved being a mother. When her second child, Nathan, was born in September 2000, she cut back her flight schedule to the minimum. And though she no longer worked on the farm, she made sure her yard was full of flowers.

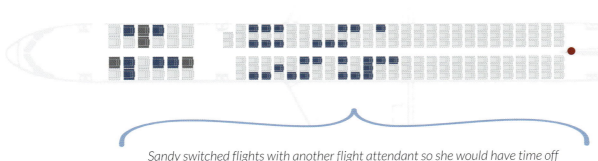

Sandy switched flights with another flight attendant so she would have time off later in September for her son's first birthday and for her class reunion.

Marion R. Britton

HOMETOWN: Brooklyn, New York /// AGE: 53 /// OCCUPATION: Assistant area director, United States Census Bureau
FAMILY: Brother, the Reverend Paul Britton; half-brother, John Britton

Marion Britton tended to be a workaholic, but often showed co-workers and people she met her generous side.

As a part-time enumerator going door-to-door for the 1980 Census, Marion came across fellow New Yorkers who fell on hard times. She felt compelled to help — even buying groceries for them.

Her generosity, though, "was sometimes balanced by sharpness," said her brother, the Reverend Paul Britton. "She could be very caustic. She let you know what was on her mind."

She never forgot her colleagues after moving up the ranks at the Census Bureau. She helped them get promotions.

She loved going out to dinner. She dined with co-workers at unique restaurants they found while canvassing for the Census. She developed a circle of friends at a diner in Brooklyn's Bay Ridge neighborhood.

Marion never married and had no children, but delighted in finding the right gifts for her two nephews. For family gatherings, she was counted on to bring unique appetizers and desserts from restaurants and bakeries she came across while traveling.

"She was strong-willed in many ways. She lived her life the way she wanted to live her life," Britton said.

Marion and a colleague, Waleska Martinez, were traveling for work to a computer conference.

Thomas E. Burnett, Jr.

HOMETOWN: San Ramon, California /// AGE: 38 /// OCCUPATION: Senior vice president and chief operating officer, Thoratec Corporation
FAMILY: Wife, Deena Burnett Bailey; daughters, Madison, Halley and Anna Clare;
parents, Thomas and Beverly Burnett; sisters, Martha Burnett Pettee and Mary Margaret Jurgens

Tom Burnett Jr. was just as comfortable conversing with corporate executives as he was talking to the man fishing next to him.

"He just loved good conversation and challenging thought," said his wife, Deena Burnett Bailey.

An intelligent and articulate man, Tom caught people off guard with his wit. He had a presence that demanded attention. He could sell anything to anybody, and thrived leading a company that produced heart pumps because he knew so many employees depended on his success.

Tom always had a book, newspaper or magazine. He couldn't wait for his three little girls to learn to read so he could pick out books for them and have discussions.

The Minnesota native was an avid hunter and fisherman. He'd take trips with his dad to Canada to hunt moose and hunted for deer several times each year. He'd spend hours fighting swordfish while deep-sea fishing. Sundays he reserved for family trips to the beach.

He let his wife know how much he appreciated everything she did for their family. And he bragged about what a good cook she was, even though she says that wasn't true. He was, after all, a great salesman.

Tom was returning home from a business trip to New York.
Originally scheduled to take a later flight, Tom made it onto United Flight 93
so he could return to his family sooner.

William Joseph Cashman

HOMETOWN: West New York, New Jersey /// AGE: 60
OCCUPATION: Iron worker, lather and licensed welder, Local 46 Metallic Lathers and Reinforcing Ironworkers
FAMILY: Wife, Maggie

As an iron worker, lather and licensed welder, William Cashman was proud to have a hand in building the World Trade Center.

The Twin Towers stood tall above Manhattan, where Billy Cashman grew up. He and his wife, Maggie, could see them from their New Jersey apartment. She watched them collapse on September 11, 2001, while her husband fought for his life aboard Flight 93.

"If he didn't die, he would have been down there (at Ground Zero) helping them," Maggie Cashman said.

Even at 60, Billy wasn't planning retirement. He worked five days a week on construction projects. He taught welding to union apprentices.

He had a red belt in karate, but was soft-spoken and a gentleman, always holding the door open for his wife of 31 years. He didn't have children, but loved spending time with his nieces and nephews, making each feel special.

Hiking was among his favorite pastimes. On 9/11 he was on his way to California to hike with friends. And he loved America. He served as a paratrooper in the United States Army's 101st Airborne Division. Every Fourth of July, he'd decorate the couple's apartment with American flags.

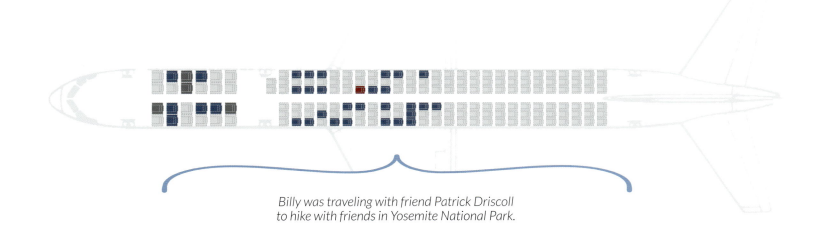

Billy was traveling with friend Patrick Driscoll to hike with friends in Yosemite National Park.

Georgine Rose Corrigan

HOMETOWN: Honolulu, Hawaii /// AGE: 55 /// OCCUPATION: Antiques dealer
FAMILY: Daughter, Laura Brough; grandchildren, Evan, Dylan and Summer Rose, born after her grandmother's death; brothers, Robert E. Marisay Jr. and Kevin Marisay

Georgine Rose Corrigan was a single mom working at a bank in Toledo, Ohio, when a chance encounter with a client led to a job at a bank in Hawaii and a move to paradise.

Raising a daughter alone in a new place wasn't easy. She often worked more than one job to make sure she could provide for her daughter.

"She'd do any kind of work that came along — babysitting people, or what-have-you," said Georgine's brother, Robert E. Marisay Jr. "Rural American people, we have a pretty good work ethic."

Georgine grew up with two brothers in Ohio along the Portage River, which became a skating rink when winter arrived. They'd play hockey using an empty can as a puck. Her parents passed along a love for antiques. Their father used to say they owned everything made in 1930 and had three of them. She parlayed that love for antiques into a business.

"Everybody who met her loved her instantly," daughter Laura Brough said. "She was very receptive, very warm, very funny. She gave the best massages."

On the one-year anniversary of 9/11, Georgine's family brought 40 lei to the crash site to honor each passenger and crew member, and brought Hawaiian Kona coffee for the families. Coffee was one of Georgine's favorite things.

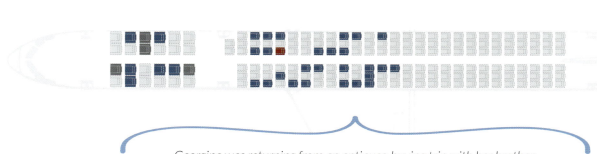

Georgine was returning from an antiques-buying trip with her brother Kevin in New Jersey. Originally scheduled for another flight, she took an open spot on Flight 93 to minimize layovers.

Patricia Cushing

HOMETOWN: Bayonne, New Jersey /// AGE: 69 /// OCCUPATION: Retired customer service representative for New Jersey Bell
FAMILY: Sons, Thomas, John and David; daughters, Alicia Cohen and Pegeen Cushing; grandchildren, Ilana and Jake Cohen and Thomas Anthony Cushing, who was born after her death.

Patricia Cushing sometimes was mother and father to her five children.

With her husband, Thomas, busy running the family's liquor store, she managed the household by herself. She got the kids to church on Sundays and to their activities. She attended their games and made sure she and her children ate dinner as a family, even if her husband couldn't be there.

"She was just very devoted to us. That was her life. We were her life, growing up," said her daughter, Alicia Cohen.

Patricia loved holidays, and she hosted the extended family get-togethers. Her children, even as adults, got home-cooked birthday dinners.

Good manners and proper English were important to her. When her husband's business wasn't doing well, she went to work at the phone company to help with the family budget.

She'd relax by watching M*A*S*H — her favorite television show. She loved doing crossword puzzles and reading mysteries, such as Agatha Christie's. She played mahjong and loved going to the opera.

When her husband died in 1987, she began spending more time with his sister, Jane Folger. They spent their last moments together aboard Flight 93.

Patricia was traveling to San Francisco with her sister-in-law, Jane Folger, for a vacation.

Jason M. Dahl

HOMETOWN: Littleton, Colorado /// AGE: 43 /// OCCUPATION: Standards captain, United Airlines
FAMILY: Wife, Sandy; son, Matthew; stepdaughter, Jennifer Blackford; stepgranddaughters, Makayla Blackford, born before his death, and Naomi and Olivia Blackford, who were born after his death.

When Jason Dahl had the chance to win flying lessons through an essay contest, he entered. He won, and earned his pilot's license before he could drive a car.

By age 27, Jason had a job with United Airlines. Within eight years he was a captain, and his young age and boyish looks earned him the nickname "Captain Doogie," a reference to the television show about the teenaged genius who became a doctor.

Despite his schedule as a pilot, Jason made time for his son's and stepdaughter's events. They celebrated every achievement with cakes and special dinners. He served as a Little League coach and Boy Scout leader.

Jason designed and built furniture and even light fixtures. He gutted the family home and remodeled it himself, building closets with automatic lights and a custom steam shower. A planned small pond in the yard became a much larger water feature that neighbors dubbed "Lake Sandy," after his wife.

Jason planned a surprise fifth anniversary party for his wife and a gift of a baby grand piano that arrived at her door days after his death.

"He lived every day like it was going to be his last," Sandy Dahl said. "He always thought of other people."

Jason switched flights with another captain so he could be home in time to take his wife on a fifth anniversary trip to London.

Joseph DeLuca

HOMETOWN: Ledgewood, New Jersey /// AGE: 52
OCCUPATION: Computer program designer, Pfizer Consumer Healthcare
FAMILY: Sister, Carol Hughes

Joe DeLuca loved cars.

All of his adult life, he was involved in auto sports. He started out in the 1960s and '70s running road rallies. By 1980, he joined the Sports Car Club of America to try his hand at racing.

His pride and joy was a bright yellow 1962 Morgan. He was president of a local club of Morgan owners and drew cartoons for its newsletter, 'Pole Position.' A cat lover, Joe created a cartoon about a race-loving cat named Raymond.

By day, Joe worked on computer systems — a trade he taught himself. He loved to travel and learn about other cultures. Though a gentle giant, he wasn't a pushover.

"He always had a sense of humor about everything, and I think it made people happy to be around him," said his sister, Carol Hughes.

He was a good son, too. After his mother had two strokes, Joe hired a nurse and made sure his parents got their medications. He handled their paperwork and bills.

Joe knew Linda Gronlund for 20 years through their interest in racing. They had been dating about six months when she invited him to go with her on a work trip to San Francisco and make it a vacation into wine country.

Joe seemed to be falling in love.

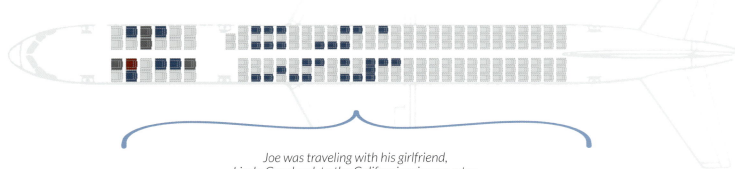

Joe was traveling with his girlfriend,
Linda Gronlund, to the California wine country.

Patrick Joseph Driscoll

HOMETOWN: Manalapan, New Jersey /// AGE: 70
OCCUPATION: Retired executive director of software development, Bell telephone companies
FAMILY: Wife, Maureen; sons, Steve, Patrick and Chris; daughter, Pamela Gould; seven grandchildren

Patrick Joseph Driscoll grew up in Manhattan's Upper East Side, but he came to love hiking in the mountains. Bryce Canyon, Yosemite and Crater Lake national parks were some of his favorite haunts, but he loved walking or hiking anywhere.

"He liked having some solitude, and he liked the peace and quiet," said his son, Chris Driscoll.

One of his favorite places to visit was his parents' homeland in Ireland. He visited distant cousins and helped them work the Driscoll farm, which has been around for generations.

Known to everyone as Joe, he was a Navy veteran and graduated first in his class at New York University's School of Engineering. He earned a master's degree from Rutgers University in computer engineering, but he hung out with blue-collar guys from his old neighborhood.

He pushed his kids to do their absolute best, but he balanced that by being there to protect and provide for them.

He and his wife, Maureen, met at the Jersey shore in the summer of 1958 and married the following summer. Days before he boarded Flight 93, they sold their house and were waiting for their new home to be built.

They were living in a rental in Point Pleasant, New Jersey. It is near the shore.

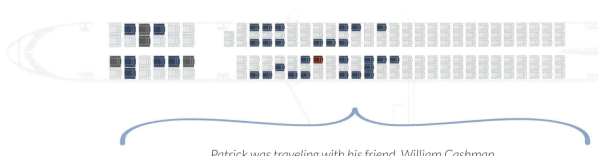

Patrick was traveling with his friend, William Cashman, to hike in Yosemite National Park.

Edward Porter Felt

HOMETOWN: Matawan, New Jersey /// AGE: 41 /// OCCUPATION: Technical director, BEA Systems Incorporated
FAMILY: Wife, Sandra; daughters, Adrienne and Kathryn; mother, Shirley Felt;
brother and sister-in-law, Gordon and Donna Felt; and brother, Larry Felt

Edward Felt always had ideas.

And he'd jot them down immediately — on a restaurant napkin, a scrap of paper, or in a notebook pulled from his wife's purse. A computer program designer, Ed invented things that made everything work. He held patents for encryption technology that offered security to computer systems.

"He got to be creative in a field that was still being developed and was constantly changing, and that just fueled his passion and his imagination," said his wife, Sandra Felt.

He made sure to spend one-on-one time with his daughters. A morning person, Ed got up even earlier to feed them when they were babies. As they got older, breakfast became their time with dad.

He had a way of making his wife laugh. Despite their different upbringings — she was a city girl, he grew up in the country — they had similar personalities.

He never called attention to himself, but always stood out. Sandra Felt knew her husband had walked into a room even before she saw him, because they had such a strong connection.

"Sandy, if my life were to end today," he once told her, "I want to make sure that it was a good day and that everybody around me knows that they were loved."

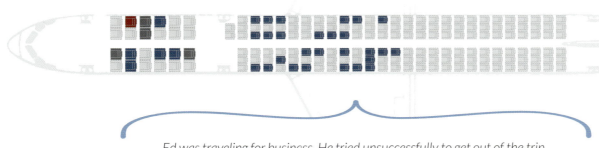

Ed was traveling for business. He tried unsuccessfully to get out of the trip.

Jane C. Folger

HOMETOWN: Bayonne, New Jersey /// AGE: 73 /// OCCUPATION: Retired bank officer
FAMILY: Sons, Robert, Thomas and Michael; daughter, Kathleen Kulik; six grandchildren

Jane Folger's son hears stories about his mother — how she always had a good word for her neighbors; how, at her bank job, she never hesitated to help people with financial troubles.

"She was very popular and just helped anybody who needed help," Robert Folger said.

For a while, Jane was a stay-at-home mom. But when her youngest child entered school, she took a job as a bank teller and worked her way up to become an officer. Working outside home helped her take control of her life, and she found the strength to leave an alcoholic husband.

"I really liked the person she became as she got older," Folger said.

Jane suffered through the devastating loss of two sons — Jackie in the Vietnam War, and Terrence from AIDS. Terrence's death hit her especially hard because she was his caretaker. She bounced back a bit when her sister-in-law, Patricia Cushing, retired, and the two spent more time together.

Jane liked to visit Manhattan. A frugal person, she'd take walking tours, visit museums and go window-shopping. She took her grandchildren in pairs to see the sights. The family cherishes a 1998 photo of her and her granddaughters at the top of the World Trade Center.

Jane was traveling to San Francisco for a vacation with her sister-in-law, Patricia Cushing.

Colleen L. Fraser

HOMETOWN: Elizabeth, New Jersey /// AGE: 51
OCCUPATION: Executive director, Progressive Center for Independent Living; vice chairwoman, New Jersey Developmental Disabilities Council
FAMILY: Sister, Christine; brother, Bruce James; stepsisters, Barbara Williams and Kay Roy; stepbrother, Mark Boyle

Colleen Fraser stood 4 feet, 6 inches tall, but in advocating for those with disabilities, she was a giant.

"Little, but loud," she made her mark nationally. She was a member of a committee that honed final details of the Americans with Disabilities Act. She got the attention of former New Jersey Governor James Florio and the late Massachusetts Senator Edward Kennedy.

"She was very determined about making change," said her sister, Christine Fraser. "If she saw that a change could be made, she would get people going."

Born with a bone disease, Fraser endured 31 surgeries during her life. A talented artist, she turned beach driftwood into beautiful objects. She once carved a Nativity scene for a friend. She loved wearing shawls and lots of jewelry. She wore her flaming red hair cut to about an inch long. Colleen loved to cook, but rarely used recipes.

She got her driver's license later in life and appreciated the freedom it brought. She'd set out in her Honda sports coupe with no destination in mind. After she died, nobody could get the car started — not even a mechanic.

"She left, and the car went too," her sister said.

Colleen was traveling to Reno, Nevada, for a grant-writing seminar to help people with disabilities obtain money to live in the community with assistance.

Andrew "Sonny" Garcia

HOMETOWN: Portola Valley, California /// AGE: 62 /// OCCUPATION: President and founder, Cinco Group Incorporated
FAMILY: Wife, Dorothy Garcia Bachler; daughters, Kelly Arrillaga and Audrey Olive; son, Andrew; grandchildren, Madisen and Sonny Garcia, Shea and Chase Arrillaga, Andrew Jacob (A.J.) and Dylan Olive. All but Madisen were born after 9/11.

When Andrew Garcia worked at his father's grocery store as a boy, his father showed him by example how to live his life.

A shoplifter tried to steal an item. Instead of calling police, Andy's father calmly told the thief: "Don't steal from me. If you're hungry, I will give you something."

"That's the caring heart, the helpfulness that was instilled in Andy at a young age by his dad," said Andy's wife, Dorothy Garcia Bachler.

Andy — whose family called him Sonny — worked his way through San Jose State University by being a mailman. He started an industrial equipment business with his wife in 1991. He exercised religiously, following a regime that included jumping rope and jumping jacks.

A practical joker, he'd sometimes call his wife on the phone, pretending to be someone else. Usually, she'd fall for it.

A member of the California Air National Guard in the 1960s, Andy started flight training but became an air traffic controller for the Guard instead. He instilled his love of airplanes in his daughter, Kelly, who would get her pilot's license. They loved to watch planes landing at San Jose's airport. They knew the make of every plane in the sky.

Andrew was returning home from a business meeting.

Jeremy Logan Glick

HOMETOWN: Hewitt, New Jersey /// AGE: 31 /// OCCUPATION: Sales executive, Vividence Incorporated
FAMILY: Wife, Lyz Glick Best; daughter, Emerson; parents, Joan and Lloyd Glick;
sisters, Jennifer and Joanna; brothers, Jonah, Jared and Jed

Jeremy Glick spent the last three months of his life soaking up precious moments with his baby daughter, Emerson. He thrived on feeding, diapering and dressing her.

"When he did something, he put his heart and soul into it," said his wife, Lyz Glick Best.

An outgoing guy with a fantastic sense of humor, Jeremy didn't take life, or himself, too seriously. He was an accomplished athlete, and won a national judo championship while at the University of Rochester. He played soccer and lacrosse, and was a wrestler. He loved learning. He was well-read on all sorts of topics.

"He was just a very well-rounded, balanced person who had priorities at a young age when people are trying to figure that out," Glick Best said.

Despite his many talents, he remained humble. He loved his job as a salesman for an Internet company because it enabled him to work from home and provide balance in his life.

He and his wife named Emerson after Jeremy's favorite poet, Ralph Waldo Emerson. She looks like her father and plays the violin, as he did. When Emerson had to pick a hero for an essay project, her choice was easy.

She wrote about her dad.

Jeremy was traveling for business and originally scheduled to fly the night before. A fire at Newark airport rerouted his flight to Kennedy Airport. He decided to take Flight 93 the next morning.

Kristin White Gould

HOMETOWN: New York City /// AGE: 65 /// OCCUPATION: Medical journalist
FAMILY: Daughter, Allison Vadhan; three grandchildren

Not one to shrink from danger, Kristin White Gould once talked a man out of mugging her, said her daughter, Allison Vadhan.

So when United Flight 93 was hijacked on September 11, 2001, "I can see her telling (a fellow passenger), 'Grab your butter knife.' She would not be huddling, weeping," her daughter said.

Kristin was a medical journalist and author, who published under the name Kristin White. Her interests ranged from philosophy to British history to exploring Roman ruins.

"She opened the doors of the world to me and to my kids with her amazing take on what was important. She brought to our family a very high standard when it came to regarding history and using our own individual intelligence to make a difference," Vadhan said. *"She had a way of painting a picture with words and making her ideas come alive to others with her vocabulary and her enthusiasm."*

Kristin taught herself to read at age 3. She was writing a book about the medical and scientific contributions of Ivy League university graduates when she died. She loved her New York lifestyle, going to plays and concerts, and she celebrated her 65th birthday in style with a party on August 30.

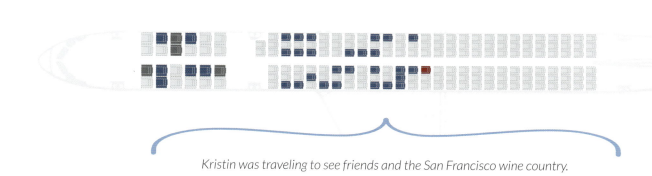

Kristin was traveling to see friends and the San Francisco wine country.

Lauren Catuzzi Grandcolas

HOMETOWN: San Rafael, California /// AGE: 38 /// OCCUPATION: Account executive for Good Housekeeping magazine
FAMILY: Husband, Jack; parents, Lawrence and Barbara Catuzzi; sisters, Dara Ann Near and Vaughn Catuzzi Lohec

Lauren Catuzzi Grandcolas was working on two wonderful projects.

She and her husband, Jack, were expecting their first child after 10 years of marriage, and she was writing a book intended to inspire women.

On September 11, 2001, returning to California from her grandmother's funeral in New Jersey, she called her husband from United Flight 93, leaving a message about a problem on the plane.

" 'I love you more than anything. Just know that.' Those were her words," said Jack Grandcolas, who has not remarried. "Lauren was my love," he said. "I haven't really gotten over that."

Lauren's father, Larry Catuzzi, called his daughter a free spirit who enjoyed roller blading, skiing and kayaking. A graduate of the University of Texas, she had 15 years of marketing and sales experience.

After her death, her family established the Lauren Catuzzi Grandcolas Foundation, which contributes to scholarships and hospital neonatal units.

Lauren's sisters, Dara Ann Near and Vaughn Catuzzi Lohec, finished her book. Published in 2005, it is titled: 'You Can Do It!: The Merit Badge Handbook for Grown-Up Girls.'

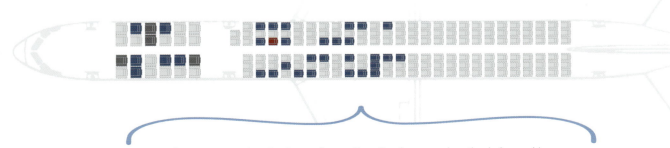

Lauren was returning home from attending her grandmother's funeral in Carlstadt, New Jersey. Flight 93 had an earlier departure than her scheduled flight.

Wanda Anita Green

HOMETOWN: Linden, New Jersey /// AGE: 49 /// OCCUPATION: Flight attendant, United Airlines
FAMILY: Daughter, Jennifer; son, Joseph; parents, Francis and Aserene Smith; a sister; a brother

Wanda Green had a way of soothing troubled souls.

As a deacon with The Linden Presbyterian Church in Linden, New Jersey, she was particularly gifted at visiting sick people in hospitals, said Rev. Dr. William C. Weaver, her pastor. At her memorial service, fellow flight attendants said they could count on her to pitch in and help with unruly passengers.

"She was always a very upbeat person. When she walked in, her smile just lit up the room," Weaver said.

Wanda was a flight attendant for 29 years. Her mother, Aserene Smith, said Wanda was one of the first black flight attendants for United Airlines. Wanda socialized with a group of mothers who planned outings together, often with their children.

Wanda's daughter, Jennifer, is a licensed emergency medical services professional, Weaver said.

"Joe is a police officer. He loves law enforcement. He was headed that way, anyway. But after talking with law enforcement officers after September 11, that confirmed his resolve," Weaver said.

Wanda earned her real estate license and planned to take up a second career after retiring from the airline. Outside her church, a tree stands in her memory. It is a weeping cherry tree.

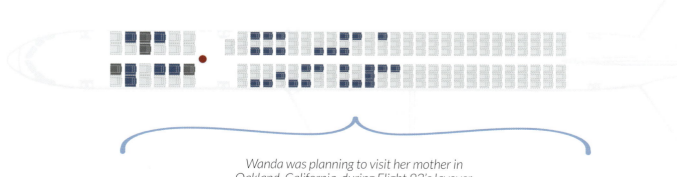

Wanda was planning to visit her mother in Oakland, California, during Flight 93's layover.

Donald Freeman Greene

HOMETOWN: Greenwich, Connecticut /// AGE: 52 /// OCCUPATION: CEO and first vice president, Safe Flight Instrument Corporation
FAMILY: Wife, Claudette; son, Charles; daughter, Jody; 11 siblings

Donald F. Greene learned to fly at age 14. He headed a family business that manufactured aviation performance and safety equipment, and some instruments on United Flight 93 came from that company, the Safe Flight Instrument Corporation.

Were Don, a licensed pilot, able to make it into the cockpit of the hijacked Boeing 757, "We all thought he was probably capable of landing that plane, and he would have made that known," said his brother, Steve Greene.

"He would have been their ace-in-the-hole. I think the passengers would have tried to get him in there," he said.

Don enjoyed piloting the company plane, his brother said.

"He had a couple of little boats, a sailboat and motorboat he liked to take out," Greene said.

Don graduated in 1971 from Brown University, where he wrestled and earned a degree in engineering. He earned a master's of business administration from Pace University.

Greene recalled an adventure from almost 40 years ago that began after he bought a piece of property in Vermont. He convinced Don and several high school buddies to come up and help him build a house. During the construction work, Greene said, chuckling at the memory, "we lived in a renovated school bus."

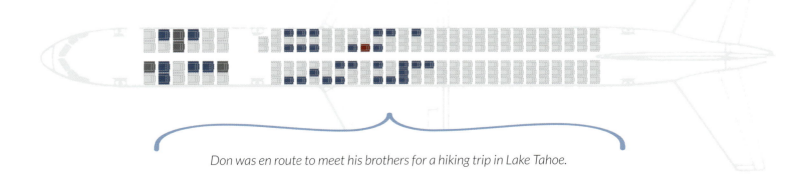

Don was en route to meet his brothers for a hiking trip in Lake Tahoe.

Linda Gronlund

HOMETOWN: Greenwood Lake, New York /// AGE: 46
OCCUPATION: Manager of environmental compliance for BMW North America
FAMILY: Parents, Doris and the late Gunnar Gronlund; sister, Elsa Strong; two nephews

Linda Gronlund knew her way around cars. She was a skilled mechanic and loved sports car racing. She even flagged races.

She was a lawyer, a certified emergency medical technician, a volunteer with a horseback riding program for autistic children, earned a brown belt in karate — and she planned to take piano lessons.

"She was an amazing, full-of-life person who lived her life. She fit a lot in," said her sister, Elsa Strong.

Linda was flying to San Francisco with her boyfriend, Joseph DeLuca. She called her sister the morning of 9/11 to pass along her flight number.

"We said, 'I love you' and 'Goodbye.' Lucky for me that was always what we said," Strong recalled.

A second call, placed from the plane, went to Strong's answering machine. Strong saw the message light at the same time her television screen flashed "Flight 93" and "No survivors."

Linda in her message explained that her flight was hijacked. Passengers were aware other planes crashed into the World Trade Center.

"She said she loved me, mom and dad and that she wasn't sure she would get to tell me again. She told me where her papers were and the combination to her safe. That was Linda. When there was a crisis, she got serious."

Linda was flying to San Francisco for a work trip and then to celebrate her 47th birthday in California wine country with her boyfriend, Joseph DeLuca.

Richard J. Guadagno

HOMETOWN: Eureka, California /// AGE: 38
OCCUPATION: Project leader and refuge manager, Humboldt Bay National Wildlife Refuge, United States Fish and Wildlife Service
FAMILY: Parents, Jerry and Bea Guadagno; sister, Lori Guadagno

Family members called Richard Guadagno their Renaissance Man. A federal law enforcement officer and refuge manager with the United States Fish and Wildlife Service, he enjoyed cooking, a skill he learned from his grandmother. Hobbies included gardening, scuba diving and mountain climbing, said his father, Jerry Guadagno.

"He collected and polished stones. He was a self-taught furniture maker and self-taught taxidermist. His latest interest was astronomy. He was a serious musician. He played piano, then he got into guitars. We found he had eight guitars, one of which was a bass guitar he made," his father said.

His son grew orchids in his kitchen and tended bonsai plants.

"He had his own greenhouse. His signature wherever he went was acres of wildflowers. I always said he could grow a garden from stone," Guadagno said.

The headquarters and visitors center at Humboldt Bay National Wildlife Refuge in Loleta, California, a building whose construction he oversaw, bears his name.

Jerry Guadagno drove his son to Newark International Airport on September 11 for his flight.

"The last thing I said to him was, 'Richard, make sure you call us when you get there.'"

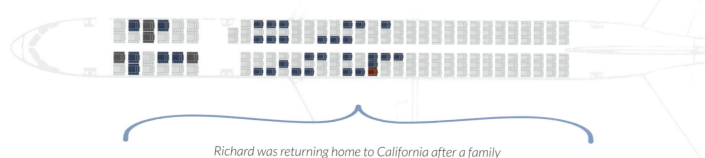

Richard was returning home to California after a family celebration for his grandmother's 100th birthday.

LeRoy W. Homer, Jr.

HOMETOWN: Long Island, New York /// AGE: 36 /// OCCUPATION: Pilot with United Airlines
FAMILY: Wife, Melodie; daughter, Laurel; parents, Ilse Homer and the late LeRoy W. Homer;
three sisters; four half-sisters; one half-brother

At age 2, LeRoy W. Homer looked into the sky and asked his parents how planes stayed up there. By 14, Homer was working to pay for flying lessons. He earned his pilot's license at 16.

"He would tell me, when he was flying, 'Mom, I always feel like I'm so close to God,'" said Ilse Homer.

He graduated in 1987 from the United States Air Force Academy and served in Operation Desert Shield and Operation Desert Storm. He flew humanitarian missions to Somalia.

His career with United Airlines began in 1995, but LeRoy continued serving in the United States Air Force Reserves. In 2008, the operations building at the Wright-Patterson Air Force Base in Ohio was named in his honor.

LeRoy enjoyed skiing, biking, roller-blading, tennis, water polo, fencing and golf. He often brought his mother her favorite perfume, Chanel No. 5, from his trips around the world.

"The last time I saw him, he was feeding Laurel. He said, 'Are you Daddy's little girl? Do you love Daddy as much as I love you?'" Homer said.

"He found the right lady and had the most beautiful little girl, and then God took him," she said. "We will never know why."

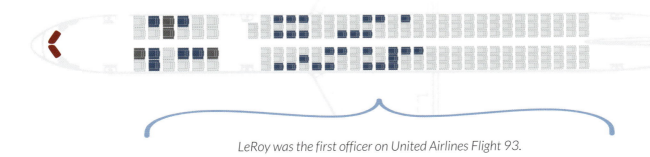

LeRoy was the first officer on United Airlines Flight 93.

Toshiya Kuge

HOMETOWN: Toyonaka City, Japan /// AGE: 20
OCCUPATION: Student, School of Science and Engineering, Waseda University, Tokyo
FAMILY: Parents, Hajime and Yachiyo Kuge; brother, Naoya

Armed with a cheerful, outgoing personality, Toshiya Kuge left Japan on August 27, 2001, for the United States and Canada.

"He decided to take a trip alone because he was eager to soak up the nature of the Canadian Rocky Mountains," said his mother, Yachiyo Kuge.

He wanted to hone his English. A student of engineering at Waseda University, Tokyo, he wanted to pursue a master's degree at a university in the United States. Toshiya loved to play and watch soccer. He loved American football and played as a linebacker during his first year on Waseda University's American football team.

"His kind heart continues to live within us to date. I will never forget his smile, kindness, genuine character and his eagerness to understand others," his mother said.

Toshiya enjoyed music and books, and had a beloved Siberian husky. Stops during his North American trip included Jasper National Park in Canada, Niagara Falls and New York City. Before leaving Japan, he wrote an entry into a guidance book about studying abroad. The events of 9/11 make his words especially poignant: "An action is more important than thinking — rather, that is the condition (for one's accomplishment)."

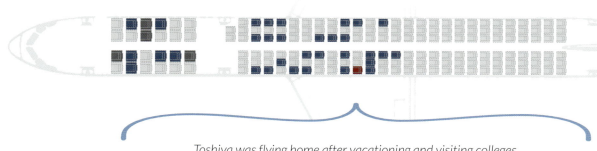

Toshiya was flying home after vacationing and visiting colleges in the United States and Canada.

CeeCee Ross Lyles

HOMETOWN: Fort Pierce, Florida /// AGE: 33 /// OCCUPATION: Flight attendant, United Airlines
FAMILY: Husband, Lorne; sons, Jerome Smith, Jevon Castrillo, Justin and Jordan Lyles; mother, Shirley Adderly; adoptive mother, Carrie Ross; aunts, Frances Watson, Mareya Schneider and Pinkie Miller; brothers, Tony Ross and William Adderly

As a member of Fort Pierce Police Department in Florida, CeeCee Ross Lyles was a natural leader, recalls colleague Dennis McWilliams. That leadership extended to her family, as well.

"She was like a go-between, a bond, a glue that kept all of us together," said her aunt, Frances Watson.

In 2000, CeeCee, a single mother, married fellow police officer Lorne Lyles. CeeCee and her husband each had two sons. The families blended well, Watson said. Soon after her marriage, CeeCee, left her job as a detective to pursue a childhood dream of becoming a flight attendant.

She was happy in her new life, her family said. In August 2001, CeeCee, her husband and sons took a vacation. She called her mother, Shirley Adderly, from the road.

"You could tell they were the happiest people on Earth. I think God gave her some of the happiest days of her life before this happened," Adderly said.

McWilliams, a sergeant with the Fort Pierce Police Department, said he believes CeeCee likely participated in the passengers' attempt to re-take the plane.

"I'm sure that CeeCee helped to prevent that plane from getting to Washington, D.C. She is a hero," he said.

Since 2002, her family has offered the CeeCee Ross Lyles Memorial Scholarship to deserving high school students in their community.

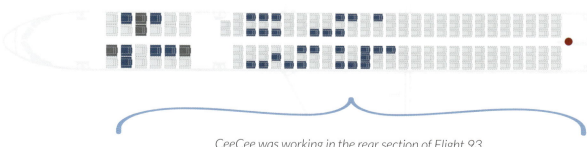

CeeCee was working in the rear section of Flight 93.

Hilda Marcin

HOMETOWN: Irvington, New Jersey /// AGE: 79
OCCUPATION: Retired special education aide from the Tinc Road School in Mount Olive, New Jersey
FAMILY: Daughters, Carole O'Hare and Elizabeth Kemmerer; granddaughter, Melissa Lata; great-grandchildren, Everett and Ellie

Hilda Marcin worked until age 79, retiring in June 2001 as an instructional aide to children with special needs.

"She loved her job. She did not take a sick day in 14 years," said her daughter, Carole O'Hare.

She moved to the United States from Germany with her parents at age 6. During World War II, Hilda worked at a Kearny, New Jersey, defense plant, seven days a week. She took one day off in February 1943 to marry her husband, Edward.

She worked for 20 years as a fund manager for a union in New Jersey. When her husband died unexpectedly during surgery in 1979, Hilda told her daughters that life was for the living.

"She said you can miss a person and love a person, but you go on with your life," O'Hare said.

After she moved to Mount Olive, New Jersey, she began working with special needs children. In her retirement, Hilda intended to split her time between O'Hare's California home and that of her other daughter, Elizabeth Kemmerer, in New Jersey. She was the oldest passenger aboard Flight 93.

"We had plans, even at her age, to volunteer together at the library and some other things," O'Hare said. "It was not her style to sit in a rocking chair."

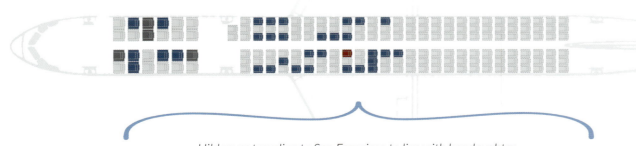

Hilda was traveling to San Francisco to live with her daughter.

Waleska Martinez

HOMETOWN: Jersey City, New Jersey /// AGE: 37 /// OCCUPATION: Automation supervisor, United States Census Bureau
FAMILY: Father, Juan Martinez; mother, Irma Martinez; half-sister, Lourdes LeBron; brother, Juan Martinez Jr.

Before leaving for a business trip on September 11, 2001, Waleska Martinez bought a present for a colleague whose birthday she would miss.

That gesture was typical of his daughter, said Juan Martinez.

"She was a really beautiful girl, inside and out," her father said. "She always liked to see everybody happy."

She remained close to her family in Puerto Rico, sometimes surprising them with visits. She loved music — Madonna and Michael Jackson were favorites — and liked to go to movies and concerts and to play softball. Her mother selected Waleska's name from a Puerto Rican actress she liked.

In her 13 years with the United States Census Bureau, she rose from clerk to automation specialist. She enjoyed her job, but did not want to go on the California trip because she didn't want to leave her mother and brother, who were visiting her in New Jersey.

After the 9/11 attacks, all flights were grounded, and Martinez could not immediately join his wife and son. Three days later, as he stood in his daughter's kitchen, he told God that he regretted being unable to give her a last embrace. Suddenly he felt Waleska's arms encircle him.

"I felt her come to me and give me a hug," he said.

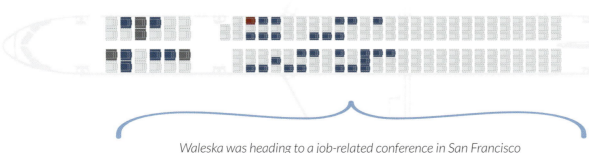

Waleska was heading to a job-related conference in San Francisco with Census Bureau colleague Marion R. Britton.

Nicole Carol Miller

HOMETOWN: San Jose, California /// AGE: 21 /// OCCUPATION: Student at West Valley College; waitress; fitness instructor
FAMILY: Father, David J. Miller; stepmother, Catherine M. Miller; mother, Cathy M. Stefani; stepfather, Wayne Stefani Sr.; siblings, Tiffney de Vries, David S. Miller, Danielle L. Miller, Wayne Stefani Jr., Joshua R.D. Tenorio and Anthony Tenorio

A picture on Nicole Carol Miller's memorial website shows her holding hands with her dad, David J. Miller, as they jumped off rocks into a creek during an August 2001 hiking trip to Upper Bidwell Park in Chico, California.

"She loved the outdoors," said her sister, Tiffney de Vries.

Energetic, blessed with a beautiful smile, Nicole was on the championship varsity swimming/diving team at Pioneer High School in San Jose and played softball, which earned her a college scholarship. She made the dean's list at West Valley College in Saratoga, but planned to transfer to California State University, either in Chico or San Jose.

"Nicole always cared about everyone else and put them ahead of herself. That's the kind of person she was," de Vries said.

It would be natural for her to give her life for another, which she did "bravely and heroically, along with the crew and passengers of United Airlines Flight 93 on September 11, 2001," said her sister.

De Vries named her daughter for Nicole. A rose was named for Nicole, too.

She had taken last-minute trip to the East Coast and was planning to return home September 10. A thunderstorm forced her to reschedule her flight.

Nicole was returning home from a trip to New York.

Louis J. Nacke, II

HOMETOWN: New Hope, Pennsylvania /// AGE: 42 /// OCCUPATION: Warehouse supervisor for K-B Toys
FAMILY: Wife, Amy; two sons from a previous marriage, Joseph Nicholas and Louis Paul III; mother, Philomena ; brothers, Ken and Dale; sister, Paula

Louis J. "Joey" Nacke II lived in quite a few places as a boy — his dad, the late Louis Paul Nacke, was transferred a lot — but the time he spent in the Pittsburgh suburb of Penn Hills made a certain impression.

"His favorite sports team was the Pittsburgh Steelers, no matter where we lived," said Kenny Nacke, although his big brother rooted for the Pirates and the Penguins, too.

As the oldest of four children, "Joey's job was to take care of us," said Nacke, who was two years younger.

His brother was generous and thought nothing of sharing with strangers. Once on a trip into Baltimore, the two saw a homeless man on a corner. Joey went into a restaurant and bought food for the man.

"He could be your best friend or your worst nightmare. You chose that. How you treated him was how he treated you," his brother said.

His brother often called out of the blue, just to check in.

"That's one of the things I think I miss the most," Nacke said.

A weightlifter, who appreciated good wine, he was married to his second wife, Amy, less than a year and was taking United Flight 93 on what was expected to be a one-day business trip to California.

Joey was flying to California for business on a last-minute trip.

Donald Arthur Peterson

HOMETOWN: Spring Lake, New Jersey /// AGE: 66
OCCUPATION: Retired owner and president of Continental Electric Company Incorporated; Christian missionary
FAMILY: Sons, David, Charles and Hamilton; grandsons, Campbell and Peyton; stepdaughters Jennifer, Grace and Catherine

Elements of Donald Peterson's took on a sense of irony after September 11, 2001.

He owned a company that manufactured electric motors. The World Trade Center had one of its products — a fire pump motor.

His longtime tennis doubles partner, Thomas Kean, a former New Jersey governor, would chair the National Commission on Terrorist Attacks Upon the United States, an independent commission that investigated the 9/11 attacks.

Don and his wife, Jean, took to missionary and counseling work in their retirement. Their pastor takes some comfort from how he believes they lived their last minutes.

"He would have had his Bible out," said Jim Loveland, of the Community Baptist Church in Neptune, New Jersey. "And they would have been ministering to the passengers. I'm certain of that."

Don volunteered at the church, taking on the most menial tasks. Hamilton Peterson said his father also volunteered with the New Jersey ministry, America's KESWICK. "He had become involved with Christian charitable work, including substance abuse counseling," Peterson said.

Don's Bible was recovered at the Flight 93 crash site with a handwritten list of men for whom he was praying.

Don and his wife were flying to San Francisco for an annual family trip with Jean's brother and parents to Yosemite National Park. They were the only married couple aboard Flight 93.

Jean Hoadley Peterson

HOMETOWN: Spring Lake, New Jersey /// AGE: 55
OCCUPATION: Retired registered nurse and nursing instructor; Christian missionary
FAMILY: Daughters, Jennifer, Grace and Catherine; stepsons, David, Charles and Hamilton; stepgrandsons, Campbell and Peyton

Jean Peterson counseled women in crisis pregnancies, volunteering for nine years with Solutions Pregnancy and Health Center in Shrewsbury, New Jersey.

She especially enjoyed mentoring mothers-to-be and choosing donated items they would need for their babies.

"She would tell them: 'You can do this,'" said center Executive Director Lorrie Erli.

Her husband, Donald, served for three years on the center's board. He often asked Erli what was on her "wish list," and then provided it.

"They made investments in people's lives, teaching people to fish rather than giving people a fish," Erli said. "They lived their lives ready to give an account. Heaven is just a better place with them there."

Jean and Don were married in 1984, each with three children from previous marriages.

Pastor Jim Loveland performed a joint memorial service for the couple, who were members of his Community Baptist Church in Neptune, New Jersey. He learned they had helped many people — not just church members — to buy homes by offering them interest-free loans.

When Jean and her husband arrived at Newark International Airport, they were offered the chance to take Flight 93 instead of their scheduled, later flight.

Jean and her husband were flying to San Francisco for an annual family trip with her brother and parents to Yosemite National Park.

Mark David Rothenberg

HOMETOWN: Scotch Plains, New Jersey /// AGE: 52 /// OCCUPATION: Owner, MDR Global Resources
FAMILY: Wife, Meredith; daughters, Sara and Rachel; two grandsons

Mark "Mickey" Rothenberg was a charming man, well-liked, friendly and outgoing.

"He had the right personality for what he did," said his wife, Meredith Rothenberg.

Her husband imported glassware and housewares, which he sold to major department stores. From reports of other passengers' cell phone calls and her own research, Rothenberg said she believes her husband was the first person the hijackers killed.

"We don't know what the reason was for that. I believe that he got involved. I have no proof. He was that kind of guy," she said.

She believes he might have tried to reason with or placate the terrorists. He quickly may have realized the passengers had to act.

"I honestly believe he was a hero," she said.

Mark grew up in Brooklyn, New York. He often traveled to Asia for his importing business. Married for 30 years to her Franklin & Marshall College sweetheart, Rothenberg said her girls adored their father.

"He was a wonderful son, an only child," she said.

Rothenberg visited the Flight 93 memorial site once, in 2002. September 11 has become a day for family.

"We try to be together. That's the best," she said.

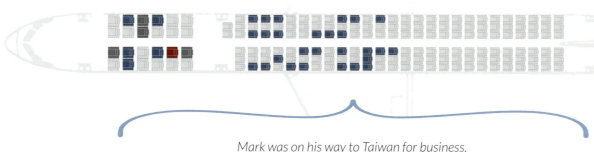

Mark was on his way to Taiwan for business.

Christine Ann Snyder

HOMETOWN: Kailua, Hawaii /// AGE: 32 /// OCCUPATION: Project manager for Outdoor Circle; arborist, certified by the International Society of Arboriculture /// FAMILY: Father, Charles O'Neal Snyder; mother, Janice Elaine Snyder; stepmother, Jan Snyder; siblings, Charles Frederick and Chad Nicholas Snyder and Lori, Tom and Dana Schaefer; partner, Ian Pescaia

Christine Snyder so loved Hawaii that she returned home after one year of college in California, said her father, Charles O'Neal Snyder.

"If she could have been at the beach every day, she would have," he said.

A certified arborist, she worked to protect trees and Hawaii's landscapes from development.

Christine attended the National Urban Forest Conference in Washington in early September and took a side trip to New York. On September 11, she was heading home. Several years ago the FBI gave the family a postcard of the World Trade Center's Twin Towers that was found in Christine's wallet at the crash site.

"She had written that she missed everybody and loved us. She was excited to get back and tell us all about it," her father said.

Christine's "promise wedding" to partner Ian Pescaia in June 2001 doubled as a family reunion, Janice Snyder said.

She recalled once accompanying her daughter to a work-related function and saw Christine easily conversing with the mayor and city officials.

"I stepped out of the box as mother and saw her potential. I had to turn away. I was in tears. It was a proud parenthood moment," she said.

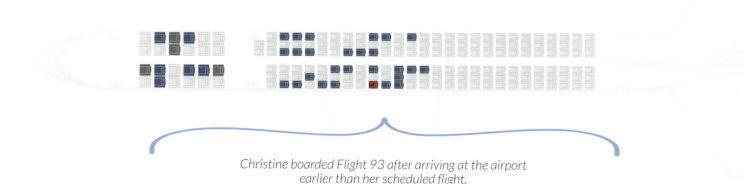

Christine boarded Flight 93 after arriving at the airport earlier than her scheduled flight.

John Talignani

HOMETOWN: Staten Island, New York /// AGE: 74 /// OCCUPATION: Retired bartender and steward, Palm restaurants, Manhattan
FAMILY: Stepsons, Mitchell and Glenn Zykofsky; sister, Alice Bertorelli

John Talignani became an instant father when he married. His wife, Selma, had three sons, and John, a gadget-loving bartender, stepped right into his new role.

"He was more than a second dad. He was a dad," said Mitchell Zykofsky, who was 19 when his mother remarried. "My younger brothers were very involved with sports. He was always involved with that."

John remained close with his stepsons after Selma died in 1997. He was going to California on United Flight 93 to claim the body of stepson, Alan, who died in a traffic accident while on his honeymoon.

The family returned to New York by driving cross-country, arriving in time to attend a Flight 93 memorial service on September 20 near the crash site. John's family members have attended each annual memorial service since then.

"We go because we have to go. It's something that we do," Zykofsky said.

John was "a hardworking, regular guy," he said, who drove a cab for a while and owned a pizzeria at one time.

"He was an avid Mets fan and an avid computer enthusiast," he said. "He had a cell phone before anyone else."

John was born in Italy and grew up in Brooklyn. He served in the United States Army during World War II.

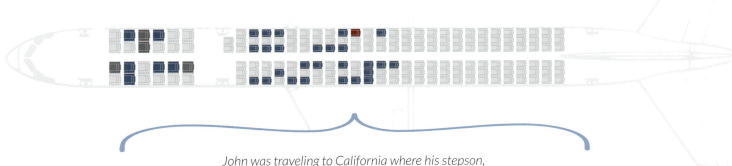

John was traveling to California where his stepson, Alan Zykofsky, had died in a car accident.

Honor Elizabeth Wainio

HOMETOWN: Watchung, New Jersey /// AGE: 27 /// OCCUPATION: District manager, Discovery Channel Store
FAMILY: Father, Ben Wainio and stepmother, Esther Heymann;
mother, Mary White, and her husband, Jay White, sister, Sarah; brother, Tom

As a student at Towson University in Maryland, Honor Elizabeth Wainio held down retail jobs to pay bills. Her mother, Mary White, said she used to secretly watch her daughter at a Gymboree store, as she played on the floor with her young customers.

"She was like her father that way, good with people," said White.

Recruited by the Discovery Channel Store, Lizz became one of its youngest district managers. She loved traveling. She returned from Europe two days before embarking on a business trip on September 11.

Lizz called her stepmother, Esther Heymann, from Flight 93 to say good-bye. Lizz's concern was for her family.

"This is going to be harder on you than on me," Heymann recalls her saying.

Lizz grew up in Baltimore and went to school in nearby Catonsville. She played all-star field hockey in high school and the viola in the all-county orchestra. She portrayed the baroness in 'The Sound of Music.'

Wainio planned to sort photos from a friend's wedding in Europe on the flight to San Francisco. The pictures were lost when the plane crashed. A friend who had traveled with her gave White a photo from their visit to France.

"She always said if she saw Paris, she would die happy," her mother said.

Lizz was headed to San Francisco for a business trip.
She changed her itinerary to board nonstop Flight 93.

Deborah Jacobs Welsh

HOMETOWN: New York City /// AGE: 49 /// OCCUPATION: Flight attendant, United Airlines
FAMILY: Husband, Patrick; mother, Lillian Jacobs

Deborah Jacobs Welsh loved the travel that being a flight attendant offered, relishing the opportunity to visit places and explore cultures.

When home in New York, she was known to take leftover airline meals and offer them to homeless people living in her Manhattan neighborhood. Nancy Meyer remembers her friend as having a "huge personality."

"She was very vibrant," she said.

Meyer and Welsh sang together in the choir of the Church of St. Paul the Apostle in New York City. For years, Meyer said, Welsh's picture hung in the choir room, surrounded by candles. She recalled Welsh and her husband, Patrick, who did scripture readings, exchanging winks during Communion.

Michael Beltran sang in the choir with Welsh. He recalled her chiding bicyclists who pedaled on city sidewalks.

"One comment that came out of her mouth all the time was, 'It's a sidewalk, not a side ride,'" he said. "It just makes me smile. I'm always cognizant of that when riding my bike in New York."

Beltran and Meyer said Welsh loved her job working for an airline. She had 25 years experience with three airlines.

"She wore her uniform, hat and all, to Mass, if she had a flight," Meyer said.

"She proudly wore those wings," Beltran said.

Deborah was assigned to first class and was responsible for overseeing the flight attendants.

"They banded together and fought back against their captors. They saved hundreds, perhaps thousands of lives. Thank God for their lives, their families and their heroism."

GOVERNOR TOM RIDGE
September 17, 2001

JUSTIN MERRIMAN

CHAPTER FOUR
INSPIRATION & MEMORY

THE GRIEVING BEGAN ALMOST IMMEDIATELY. AS PENNSYLVANIA STATE POLICE SET UP A PERIMETER AROUND THE SMOLDERING FIELD WHERE UNITED AIRLINES FLIGHT 93 WENT DOWN IN SOMERSET COUNTY, FOUR SPONTANEOUS "TRIBUTES" WENT UP NEARBY.

The crash site came to have an emotional and spiritual power similar to that experienced during a visit to Gettysburg or Antietam. The windy, barren field drew hundreds of thousands of visitors, many leaving personal items at the temporary memorial.

A group of soldiers who fought in Afghanistan left a yellow brick with this note wrapped around it:

"This brick is from the compound of Taliban leader Mullah Mohammed Omar in Kandahar, Afghanistan. On Oct. 20, 2001, U.S. Special Operations Forces attacked and seized the compound. It is now used as a U.S. base from which attacks are launched against the Taliban and al-Qaida. Placed here in tribute to the first warriors of the Global War on Terror by members of the 19th Special Forces."

The impulse to leave things where we collectively grieve is a common one. It caught on in the 1980s at the Vietnam Veterans Memorial in Washington, where the National Park Service has collected more than 100,000 items. These offerings enable ordinary people to leave their mark at a national forum.

Visitors left more than 40,000 mementos at the temporary Flight 93 memorial with its familiar chain-link fence — among the keepsakes were badges, toys, military ribbons and medals, hats, T-shirts and flowers, a flight attendant's uniform and a wedding ring.

> "You grieve today and the hurt will not soon go away. But that hope is real, and it's forever, just as the love you share with your loved ones is forever."
>
> **FIRST LADY LAURA BUSH**
> SPEAKING TO FAMILY MEMBERS AT A PRIVATE MEMORIAL SERVICE
> *September 17, 2001*

Linda Linton and her 6-year-old great-granddaughter Shyann Taylor of North Carolina visit the Flight 93 temporary memorial on July 22, 2008. The memorial gets about 130,000 visitors each year from across the United States and around the world.
JUSTIN MERRIMAN

President George W. Bush and First Lady Laura Bush commemorate the first anniversary of the 9/11 attacks on September 11, 2002, by meeting the Flight 93 families where their loved ones died. This ground is off-limits to the public, but can be viewed at a distance from the Memorial Plaza.

AP IMAGES

"We must live up to the inspiration and memory of the heroes on flight 93. They've been linked to Somerset County and the world in terms of history. We want to make sure in anything we do that we act with the same purpose and direction they did."

SUSAN HANKINSON
SOMERSET COUNTY CONSULTANT

preparing for the first anniversary

President George W. Bush and first lady Laura Bush lay a wreath on September 11, 2002, at the site where Flight 93 crashed.

AP IMAGES

Alice Hoaglan gives a hug during a visit to the temporary memorial on September 11, 2003. Her son, Mark Bingham, was a passenger on the plane. Hoaglan of San Francisco spent several hours visiting with volunteers, who act as ambassadors for visitors. At the time visitors numbered 7,000 each week.

JUSTIN MERRIMAN

GUY WATHEN

A large American flag drapes the Somerset County Courthouse and luminaria for each of the Flight 93 passengers and crew adorn the courthouse steps as part of a memorial service on September 14, 2001. More than 1,500 people attend the service.

John Paul McConnell of New Castle, Pennsylvania, participates in a candlelight service on September 10, 2002, at the Flight 93 Memorial Chapel in Stonycreek. Crews that afternoon completed work to convert the old country church building-turned-seed distribution center into a private, nondenominational chapel.

SCOTT SPANGLER

JUSTIN MERRIMAN

The Memorial Kite Project simultaneously honors 9/11 victims in New York, Washington and Somerset County on September 11, 2003. Stacy Brancato of Pittsburgh participates by flying a kite in a field near the Flight 93 crash site.

Constance Hasenei of Columbia, Maryland, lost her great-aunt Patricia Cushing on Flight 93. Constance, 5, listens to officials discuss plans on September 11, 2004, for a competition to select the design for the Flight 93 National Memorial.

ERIC SCHMADEL

A United Airlines flight attendant visits the memorial on the first anniversary of the crash.

SCOTT SPANGLER

A guest book in the ambassador's station at the temporary Flight 93 memorial awaits visitors' signatures on August 19, 2005

BRIAN F. HENRY

Rosary beads hang from a cross on September 10, 2002, at the temporary memorial.

Yachiyo Kuge, mother of Toshiya Kuge, a passenger on Flight 93, is comforted by Karel Castel of Johnstown. Kuge was visiting the temporary memorial on the fourth anniversary of the crash.

JUSTIN MERRIMAN

GUY WATHEN

Flight 93 family members attend a memorial service on September 11, 2006, at PNC Park during a game with the Milwaukee Brewers. The Pirates pay tribute to the Flight 93 passengers and crew, and fans sing "God Bless America" during the seventh-inning stretch.

CHRISTOPHER HORNER

The release of 40 white doves during a service at the temporary memorial marks the sixth anniversary of the crash.

SCOTT SPANGLER

GUY WATHEN

Relatives of CeeCee Ross Lyles attend the memorial service commemorating the eighth anniversary of the crash. CeeCee was a flight attendant on the plane. From left, Lee Mills, Denise Mills, Shirley Adderly and Frances Watson observe a moment of silence.

Matt Deal of Phoenix, Arizona, visits the temporary memorial on July 6, 2010. The flags are at half-staff to honor United States Senator Robert Byrd of West Virginia, who died at age 92 on June 28, 2010, and was buried on July 6.

GUY WATHEN

Joyce Bender of East Palestine, Ohio, takes a photograph while visiting the temporary memorial on July 6, 2010.

Flight 93 family members participate in a moment of remembrance during the Steelers' season opener against the Tennessee Titans on September 10, 2009, at Heinz Field.

CHRISTOPHER HORNER

ERIC SCHMADEL

Jerry Guadagno accepts an American flag in honor of his son, Richard J. Guadagno, during a ceremony on July 15, 2010, to name part of Pennsylvania State Game Lands 93 as the Richard J. Guadagno Habitat Area and Nature Trail. The 669-acre game lands, located at the northern boundary of the Flight 93 memorial, honors the passengers and crew.

Danielle Aponte of North Plainfield, New Jersey, stands at the temporary memorial with an American flag on the seventh anniversary of the 9/11 attacks. She and fellow cheerleaders at North Plainfield High School spend the day visiting all three sites in Washington, New York and Somerset County, Pennsylvania.

GUY WATHEN

Rain-soaked roses rest on a wooden bench at the temporary memorial during the sixth anniversary memorial service on September 11, 2007. The benches are dedicated to the Flight 93 passengers and crew members.

SCOTT SPANGLER

GUY WATHEN

GUY WATHEN

On September 11, 2009, Deborah Borza of Foxfire Village, North Carolina, visits the temporary memorial and spends a moment at an angel dedicated to her daughter Deora Bodley, a passenger on Flight 93. Deora was the youngest passenger on board.

79

VISITORS HAVE LEFT MORE THAN 40,000 MEMENTOS AT THE TEMPORARY MEMORIAL

This brick is from the compound of Taliban leader Mullah Mohammed Omar in Kandahar, Afghanistan. It was retrieved after United States Special Operations Forces attacked and seized the compound on October 20, 2001.

A baseball signed "Schenectady, N.Y., Blue Jays" bears this message: *"Heroism allows us to … 'Dare to dream, dare to succeed.'"* The minor league farm team folded in 1957.

This watch left in remembrance bears the insignia of the Reserve Officers Association, a professional association for all uniformed services of the United States.

Rosary beads are among the religious items left at the Flight 93 temporary memorial.

The round pin attached to this stuffed animal reads: *"In memory of those we lost, September 11, 2001."*

Members of the Shanksville Volunteer Fire Department signed this fireman's coat, which was hung on the chain-link fence. The department was the first emergency unit at the scene.

Passenger Toshiya Kuge of Japan was a huge fan of American football. The note on this Steelers hat is addressed to him: *"We thank you for your courage."*

Purple Heart recipient Tom Walker left his medal on May 20, 2006, pinned to a leather motorcycle vest.

The Carlson family of Monroeville left this flag on June 29, 2002, with this message: *"Thank God for all who fight for liberty and against evil, darkness & terror."*

PHOTOS BY GUY WATHEN

A United Airlines pilot's hat was left with a handwritten note to Captain Jason Dahl that says:
"Jason, working with you was always a pleasure. Forgive me for not making it here sooner, but I just was not able to do it. You have a 'salute and release from guidance' for the final time. Happy flying, Capt. Brett Anderson."

All items left at the temporary memorial, including these small flags that contain personal messages, are archived and put in storage.

Andrea Kuba of Pittsburgh put this message on a Steelers license plate:
"To the heroes of Flight 93, thank you for defending my freedom! May God's perpetual light shine upon you."

This angel figurine bears a handwritten *"... thank you."*

Edward Cruz, CEO of E.E. Cruz, the company hired to excavate the foundation of the World Trade Center, brought pieces of bedrock from the center to the temporary memorial.

Shofars are most often made from ram's horns and traditionally are blown at Rosh Hashana, the Jewish new year. This one was left at the site.

Children from St. Paul, Minnesota, left a plaque with the message:
"Thank you for caring, fighting and dying for our future!"

Mementos include many children's toys, such as this figure of Spiderman.

The note attached to this compass says: *"Let these courageous people show us the way …"*

A metal bracelet bears the name of PFC Andrew Snarey of Pennsylvania.

This National Defense Medal, awarded to members of the Armed Forces for honorable service in the Korean, Vietnam, the gulf wars and the war on terror, was placed at the site.

Inside the brim of this sailor's hat is this message: *"Proudly defending the freedom you helped to preserve! ET3 Eric M. Alog, USNUSS Jacksonville SSN 6999/03/02."* The USS Jacksonville is a nuclear-powered submarine.

A toy plane signed by Shanksville students Andy Shelbie Carter and Dawson Snyder bears the message: *"Thank you for saving our lives & for not hitting our school."*

Badges from many police and law enforcement agencies were left. This one is from the Transportation Security Administration, established by President George W. Bush after the 9/11 attacks.

Many of the more than 40,000 tributes left at the Flight 93 temporary memorial were deposited at this chain-link fence. Items there on May 23, 2003, included flags, flowers, wreaths, ball caps and banners. The fence and the cross that stood nearby were dismantled in July 2010. They and the tributes were archived and put in storage. The temporary memorial was moved to another location to prepare for construction of the permanent memorial.
JUSTIN MERRIMAN

CHAPTER FIVE
'WE WILL FIND YOU'

AS AMERICA GRAPPLED WITH THE SHOCK AND PAIN OF THE SEPTEMBER 11, 2001, ATTACKS, MILITARY STRATEGISTS BEGAN PLANNING THE OFFENSIVE AGAINST THOSE RESPONSIBLE.

We will find you, President George W. Bush promised.

On October 7, 2001, America's longest war began. The first assault — Operation Enduring Freedom — occurred in Afghanistan. The United States led a coalition against the international terrorist group al-Qaida, whose leader Osama bin Laden coordinated the 9/11 attacks.

Operation Iraqi Freedom was launched on March 19, 2003, to liberate Iraq from dictator Saddam Hussein. United States forces found Hussein hiding in a "spider hole" in an isolated farm on December 13, 2003. He was hanged on December 30, 2006. Operation New Dawn began September 1, 2010, and marked the official end to combat operations by United States forces in Iraq. Troops remain in Afghanistan and Iraq.

More than 4,800 military men and women lost their lives in combat. More than 44,000 members of the armed forces were wounded in the fighting.

The war's financial costs have been heavy, too. The Department of Defense spent about $13 billion a month for the wars in Afghanistan and Iraq.

Unlike the 1941 attack on Pearl Harbor that drew the United States into World War II, this fight is against nationless terrorists, extremist organizations, networks and their supporters.

The United States military changed. Today the military has a greater array of tools, and the Army has been transformed, becoming more mobile and competent in counterinsurgency.

> "War has been waged against us by stealth and deceit and murder. This nation is peaceful, but fierce when stirred to anger."
>
> **PRESIDENT GEORGE W. BUSH**
> IN REMARKS TO THE NATION DURING THE NATIONAL DAY OF PRAYER AND REMEMBRANCE
> *September 14, 2001*

President George W. Bush admires the determined attitude of firefighter Bob Beckwith during a visit to the devastated World Trade Center in New York on September 14, 2001. Three days earlier, the North and South towers collapsed; four other structures near or part of the World Trade Center collapsed; three buildings partially collapsed, and eight sustained major damage.
AP IMAGES

A group of Westmoreland County emergency responders travel to New Jersey the night of September 11, 2001, to assist with rescue efforts. With the New York skyline smoldering in the background, they ride home the next day after learning that New York has all the volunteers it can handle.

GUY WATHEN

Just an instant before the second jetliner hit the south tower of the World Trade Center.

Sergeant Ryan Baumann of Great Mills, Maryland, with the 101st Airborne Division, patrols part of Khost Province in Afghanistan on May 13, 2008. He died August 1, 2008, when his Humvee hit an improvised explosive device along Route Alaska in Khost Province. He was 24.

PHOTOS BY JUSTIN MERRIMAN

An officer with the Afghanistan National Police carries a rocket-propelled grenade launcher during a May 7, 2008, joint mission with the Army's 101st Airborne Division in Kutchyan, a village in Khost Province, Afghanistan. The region sits on the border with Pakistan.

Army Private First Class Santos Moreno of San Antonio, Texas, patrols in Lagorah, a village in Khost Province, Afghanistan, in May 2008. Moreno, 21, with the 101st Airborne Division, is on a mission to find Taliban insurgents.

Soldiers with the Army's 101st Airborne Division lead suspected Taliban soldiers away for processing on May 18, 2008, after a night raid with night-imaging equipment on a home in Wum Khayal, a village in Khost Province.

Soldiers with the Army's 3rd Infantry Division conduct a re-enlistment ceremony on an oil field in Kirkuk, Iraq, on March 2, 2010. Some soldiers re-enlisted for four years; some, for six. Nearly all who re-enlisted had completed tours of duty in Iraq and Afghanistan.
JUSTIN MERRIMAN

CHAPTER SIX
JUSTICE IS DONE

THE NEARLY 10-YEAR SEARCH ENDED IN A 40-MINUTE RAID. UNITED STATES NAVY SEALS KILLED OSAMA BIN LADEN, MASTERMIND OF THE 9/11 ATTACKS, DURING A MIDDLE-OF-THE-NIGHT RAID ON HIS COMPOUND IN PAKISTAN.

The United States did not tell Pakistan about the operation in advance, for fear of tipping off the AK-47-toting extremist, who preached "death to the infidels." President Barack Obama announced bin Laden's death on May 1, 2011, saying: "Justice has been done."

The hunt for bin Laden began almost immediately after the 9/11 attacks. Army General Tommy Franks, commander in chief of the United States Central Command for the Middle East and Central Asia, was told the next day to develop and deliver to Defense Secretary Donald Rumsfeld a plan for pursuing bin Laden and his al-Qaida terrorist group. President George W. Bush promised that "we will hunt him to the ends of the Earth."

The pursuit occupied the administrations of Bush and Obama and led the United States into wars in Afghanistan and Iraq. At home, it resulted in the creation of the federal Department of Homeland Security to counter the threat of terror attacks on United States soil.

Al-Qaida was blamed for the 1998 bombings of United States embassies in Kenya and Tanzania that killed 231 people, and the attack on the USS Cole that killed 17 American sailors in Yemen in 2000, as well as countless other plots — some successful and some not. At the time of his death, bin Laden was plotting an attack on the United States for the 10th anniversary of 9/11.

> "The American people did not choose this fight. It came to our shores and started with the senseless slaughter of our citizens. After nearly 10 years of service, struggle and sacrifice, we know well the costs of war."
>
> **PRESIDENT BARACK OBAMA**
> *May 1, 2010*

United States Navy SEALs kill Osama bin Laden on May 1, 2011, during a raid in Pakistan. A visitor leaves the May 2, edition of the Tribune-Review on a chain-link fence at the United Flight 93 crash site as a tribute to the fallen passengers and crew.
GUY WATHEN

EPILOGUE
FIELD OF HONOR

WITHIN DAYS AFTER UNITED FLIGHT 93 CRASHED, PEOPLE BEGAN LEAVING FLOWERS AND TEDDY BEARS AND FLAGS NEAR THE SITE. IT SOON BECAME CLEAR THAT A PERMANENT MEMORIAL WOULD BE NEEDED TO HONOR THE 40 MEN AND WOMEN WHO GAVE THEIR LIVES.

A year later, Congress authorized the creation of the Flight 93 National Memorial, to be operated by the National Park Service.

But how best to turn a scrap yard and strip mine into a place of reverence?

Family members of victims, residents and design experts chose the work of Paul Murdoch Associates from more than 1,000 entries. The winning design accentuates the natural topography of the crash site.

Critics, though, saw parallels to a symbol of Islam and demanded changes. The 9/11 attacks were the work of Islamic extremists. Most revisions addressed site conditions and material selection. A crescent-shaped, tree-lined walkway follows a more circular path.

To be built in phases, the nearly $60 million memorial will stretch from Route 30, where a 93-foot tall Tower of Voices will mark the entrance to the memorial and contain 40 wind chimes, representing the voices of the passengers and crew.

Memorial walls will stand 40 to 50 feet high — the altitude of the plane as people saw it barreling to Earth. A visitors center inside those walls will tell the story of the heroes on board.

From there, visitors will see the Field of Honor, surrounded by 40 memorial groves, each containing 40 trees. They will be able to walk along the Memorial Plaza, etched with the names of the passengers and crew, as it follows the doomed airliner's path.

> "It's fitting of what happened that day. It's a battleground. It's a burial ground. It's a way to preserve that in a secure way and to tell the story for future generations of what happened that day in that quiet valley."
>
> **DAVID BEAMER**
> FATHER OF FLIGHT 93 PASSENGER TODD BEAMER, COMMENTING ON THE DESIGN FOR THE FLIGHT 93 NATIONAL MEMORIAL
>
> *April 25, 2011*

Shovels are readied for the groundbreaking on November 7, 2009, for the Flight 93 National Memorial. The memorial, which is being built in phases, will cost about $60 million.
GUY WATHEN

From left: Campbell and Peyton Peterson, grandsons of Flight 93 passenger Donald Arthur Peterson; Sarah Wainio, sister of passenger Honor Elizabeth Wainio; and Justin Nacke, nephew of passenger Louis J. Nacke II, participate in the Flight 93 National Memorial ground-breaking ceremony on November 7, 2009.

GUY WATHEN

People from many backgrounds pay respects to the passengers and crew of Flight 93. An Amish family visits the crash site on June 6, 2011, while construction of the permanent memorial progresses in the background.
JUSTIN MERRIMAN

Jeff Reinbold, National Park Service site manager for the Flight 93 National Memorial, looks on as architect Paul Murdoch discusses the memorial's design and construction on August 12, 2010.

A lighting fixture is readied for the memorial's dedication on the 10th anniversary of the 9/11 attacks. The first phase contains the Memorial Plaza, where people can view the crash site and leave tributes.

JARED WICKERHAM

JUSTIN MERRIMAN

The Allée, a tree-lined walkway, will encircle the Field of Honor. It will be flanked by 40 Memorial Groves in honor of each passenger and crew member, and each grove will contain 40 trees.

A distant view of the Tower of Voices as it might look in spring. The beauty of the changing seasons is an important part of the focus of the memorial.

The Entry Portal will be set along Flight 93's final path. Visitors will pass through twin openings made by walls about 40-50 feet high, which approximate the altitude of the plane as it passed overhead.

The 93-foot-tall Tower of Voices will stand at the entrance and exit of the park. It will house 40 wind chimes, whose ringing will be a reminder of the acts of courage aboard Flight 93.

The Memorial Plaza Gateway is a threshold that visitors pass through to reach the Memorial Plaza. Within it is a small glass structure, the Visitor Shelter, designed to get visitors out of the weather.

RENDERINGS: BIOLINIA & PAUL MURDOCH ARCHITECTS

"We wanted simplicity, and we wanted the crash site respected, and we wanted that to be the focal point, and that's what this design has done. They've respected the land, and they've respected what's happened here."

SANDRA FELT
WIFE OF FLIGHT 93 PASSENGER EDWARD FELT
April 8, 2011

The heart of the Flight 93 National Memorial is Sacred Ground, the Flight 93 crash site and final resting place of the 40 passengers and crew members. It will be left untouched. Only family members will have access, but Memorial Plaza gives the public a good view of it and of a hemlock grove that absorbed much of the impact of the crash. Niches in the plaza's low, sloped wall accommodate personal tributes and remembrances from visitors. Names of the passengers and crew are inscribed on a white marble wall that follows the path of the plane.

BIOLINIA & PAUL MURDOCH ARCHITECTS

"A common field one day. A field of honor forever."

WRITTEN BY STEPHEN RUDA, FORMER COMMANDER OF FIRE STATION 39 IN VAN NUYS, CALIFORNIA, ON A FLIGHT 93 MEMORIAL QUILT IN 2004 MADE BY SUZI BIRD, THE WIFE OF RETIRED CO-WORKER JIM BIRD. THE PHRASE BECAME PART OF THE PREAMBLE TO THE FLIGHT 93 NATIONAL MEMORIAL MISSION STATEMENT.

August 2004

ACKNOWLEDGEMENTS

The terrorist attacks of September 11, 2001, ended the lives of nearly 3,000 people in New York City, in Washington, D.C., and near Shanksville in Somerset County, Pennsylvania.

The attacks also changed forever the lives of the victims' families, friends and co-workers – and, in equal or lesser measures, the lives of all Americans.

Field of Honor: How Flight 93 Inspired a Nation is a tribute to those victims and their survivors, as well as to the men, women and families of our nation's military who have deployed in the continuing battle against terrorism since 9/11.

While we focus on those who died aboard Flight 93, we also examine the impact on our nation and the world, on all of us who lived through one of America's darkest days.

**MANY PEOPLE CONTRIBUTED TO THIS BOOK,
AND WE THANK THEM FOR THEIR INVALUABLE ASSISTANCE.
THEY INCLUDE:**

The family and friends of Flight 93's passengers and crew who shared stories and photos.

Carole O'Hare, daughter of Flight 93 passenger Hilda Marcin, who helped us to reach out to all Flight 93 families.

Gordon W. Felt, brother of passenger Edward Felt, who wrote the book's foreword.

Lisa Linden, chief executive officer of Linden Alschuler & Kaplan, Inc., who represented Flight 93 families.

Jeff Reinbold, site manager of the Flight 93 National Memorial, who shared his knowledge of 9/11's events, the crash of Flight 93, and the plans for a permanent memorial.

Barbara Black, curator of the Flight 93 National Memorial, who provided access to many of the thousands of mementos left at the temporary memorial and to the stories surrounding those.

Kathie Shaffer, Flight 93 oral history and documentation project assistant, who recorded 655 oral histories, including those of Flight 93's first responders,

Somerset County residents, and families of Flight 93's passengers and crew.

King Laughlin, vice president of the Flight 93 National Memorial, National Park Foundation, for helping to promote Field of Honor.

Finally, I thank the many Tribune-Review staffers whose dedication and hard work produced Field of Honor; their names are listed on the Contents page.

FRANK L. CRAIG
Editor of the Pittsburgh Tribune-Review

Construction of the permanent memorial continues on April 21, 2011, at the crash site of United Flight 93.
JUSTIN MERRIMAN

Days after Flight 93 crashed, Robert Trent watches a magnificent sunrise over his 150-acre farm in Somerset County.

SCOTT SPANGLER

REFERENCES & SOURCES

David Abshire, president of the Center for the Study of the Presidency and Congress and former U.S. ambassador to NATO

Barbara Black, curator, Flight 93 National Memorial

Diane R. Case

Paulette Curtis, museum anthropologist and assistant dean, University of Notre Dame

Tom Fazi, information and education supervisor, Pennsylvania Game Commission Southwest Region

Flight 93 Memorial Chapel

Flight 93 National Memorial

Donna Glessner, oral history and documentation project assistant, Flight 93 National Memorial

Donald Goldstein, historian and retired professor, University of Pittsburgh, co-author of 'At Dawn We Slept: The Untold Story of Pearl Harbor'

Sarah Barringer Gordon, the Arlin M. Adams Professor of Constitutional Law and professor of History at the University of Pennsylvania

Bruce Hoffman, director of the Center for Peace and Security Studies, Georgetown University

Seth Kreimer, the Kenneth W. Gemmill Professor of Law at the University of Pennsylvania Law School

King Laughlin, vice president, Flight 93 National Memorial, National Park Foundation

National Park Service

The National September 11 Memorial and Museum

National Transportation Safety Board

New York City Office of Chief Medical Examiner

New York State Museum

The 9/11 Report by The National Commission on Terrorist Attacks Upon the United States

Northern New Jersey Region of the Sports Car Club of America

'A Place of Remembrance: Official Book of the National September 11 Memorial'

The Port Authority of New York & New Jersey

Lynn Rasic, senior vice president of public affairs and communications, National September 11 Memorial and Museum

Jeff Reinbold, site manager, Flight 93 National Memorial

Andrea Schuemann

Kathie Shaffer, oral history and documentation project assistant, Flight 93 National Memorial

Brad Shober, deputy chief, Shanksville Volunteer Fire Department

Marianne Spampinato, communications manager, American Red Cross, Greater Alleghenies Region

Werner Troesken, professor of economics and economic history, University of Pittsburgh

Tribune-Review

United States Department of Defense

United States Department of Justice